Contents

Map	4
Key	6
Introduction	7
Prologue	8
The 50 Buildings	10
Acknowledgements	95

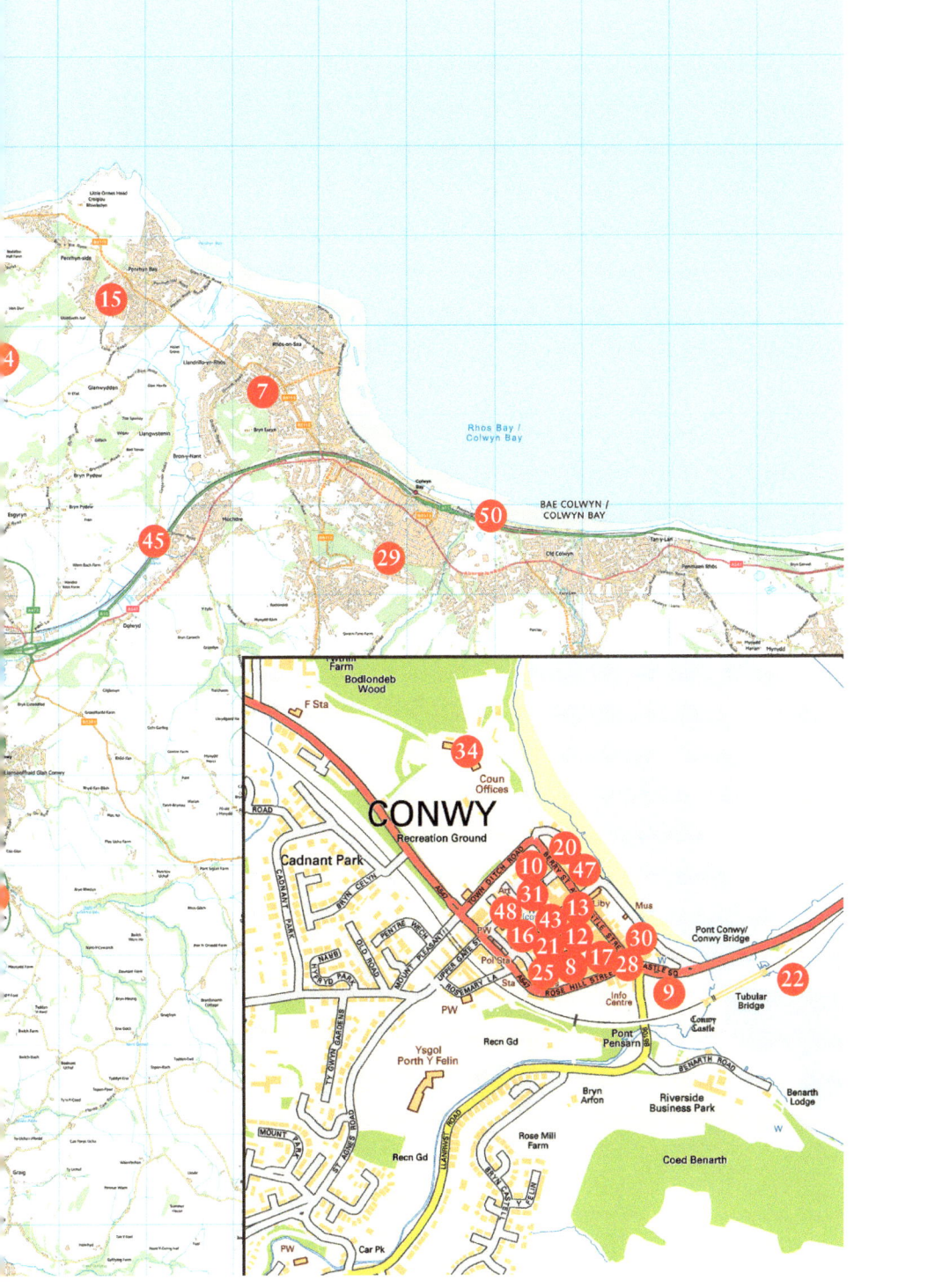

Key

1. Lletty'r Filiast
2. Barclodiad y Gawres
3. Castell Caer Seion
4. Canovium / Church
5. St Tudno's Church
6. Deganwy Castle
7. Llys Euryn
8. Canovium and St Mary's Church
9. Conwy Castle
10. Conwy town walls
11. St Benedict's Church
12. Aberconwy House
13. No. 11 Castle Street
14. Gloddaeth Hall
15. Penrhyn Old Hall
16. Plas Mawr
17. Old College
18. Bodysgallen Hall
19. Felin Isaf Mills
20. 'Smallest House'
21. Castle Hotel
22. Crossing the Conwy
23. Summit complex, Great Orme
24. New York Cottages
25. Conwy Visitor Centre
26. Grand Hotel
27. Camera Obscura
28. Guildhall
29. Plas Pwllycrochan
30. Harbourmaster's office
31. Capel Carmel
32. Llandudno Pier
33a and 33b. Toll Houses
34. Bodlondeb
35. St Paul's Church
36. Bodlondeb Castle Hotel
37. Tram Station
38. Oriel Mostyn Gallery
39. Town Hall, Llandudno
40. Emmanuel Christian Centre
41. The Close, Llanfairfechan
42. Clare's
43. Palace Cinema
44. The Round House
45. Marl Cold Store
46. Royal Artillery School
47. Parisella's Kiosk
48. Royal Cambrian Academy
49. Venue Cymru
50. Porth Eirias

Introduction

Tracing the history and development of Conwy and its environs through fifty of its significant, important or iconic buildings – what a splendid project. And how straightforward, what with Conwy's wealth of medieval and Renaissance edifices, and Llandudno's fine array of Victorian architecture amply demonstrating its growth as a modish holiday destination.

We should have known it wasn't to be that simple. To begin with, our region – roughly within the man-made boundaries of Conwy County Borough Council – covers around 1,130 square kilometres, and contains buildings and structures dating in an unbroken line from the Neolithic to last Wednesday (metaphorically speaking). So our task then became somewhat more focussed: selecting buildings that in some way represented each of the different chronological or historical periods. Our long list comprised over 200 examples; our short list was scarcely smaller. As well, we realised that many of our buildings – by dint of their iconic, even celebrity status both locally and further afield – were already abundantly described and otherwise represented in other resources elsewhere.

Our aim, then, became to provide a different perspective. We realised that history is made not by buildings, however interesting or impressive, but by people. Thus the core rationale of *Conwy & Around in 50 Buildings* began to take shape: it is not a history of the architecture of the region but rather one of the people who built, lived, worked in, and were otherwise associated with the buildings featured; thereby putting this dramatically beautiful, historically rich area into context with contemporaneous events occurring in the wider world.

Peter Johnson & Catherine Jefferis
Penmaenmawr, September 2016

Prologue

Buildings are such a permanent feature of our lives that we can forget that, for most of the history of our species, we lived with no shelter other than what nature provided, such as beneath a dark brooding tree or a precarious rock overhang. Around 45,000 years ago, in the latter stages of the Palaeolithic (the Old Stone Age), we arrived in Europe, reaching Britain about 14,000 years later. For around 16,000 years after this initial colonisation, northern Europe was subjected to great sheets of ice inexorably spreading and then receding across the landscape, grinding and washing away the traces of the few who had crossed the land bridge from mainland Europe. Any temporary shelters we erected from natural resources have long since decayed. One natural shelter, caves – and one which in certain circumstances can withstand the ravages of Ice Ages – supplies us with much that we know of our earliest ancestors. These may be considered forerunners to the buildings we use today, being a relatively stable and permanent space enclosed by walls and a roof within which specific activities and functions can take place.

Within the area covered in this book the earliest cave sites date to very late in the Palaeolithic, such as Kendrick's Cave on the Great Orme above Llandudno, which was occupied about 28,000 years ago. Unfortunately for any later residents of these caves, the ice relentlessly descended from the north again, to crush the landscape beneath for another 11,000 years; the ice retreated one last time from north Wales around 17,000 years ago.

When north Wales was again populated at the start of the Mesolithic (Middle Stone Age: approximately 12,000–5,500 years ago in north Wales), it was by people who could manufacture intricate small flint tools to aid in their nomadic hunter-gatherer existence. It has been estimated that at any one time during at least the earlier few thousand years of the Mesolithic the entire population of Wales was no more than about 300 souls. Their flint tools have been found along the coast of north Wales, but no other signs remain; most of the land they hunted upon has been lost beneath the sea. Britain during this period was a peninsular of Europe until around 8,000 years ago (6000 BC) when it became an island, probably due to a giant tsunami shattering the land-links to Europe – the final blow during an age of rising sea levels.

In the late Mesolithic there is evidence for manipulation of the environment by people who moved with the seasons from upland to lowland areas, but it is in the next period, the Neolithic (New Stone Age), that more fundamental changes can be detected. It is at this time that we begin our journey through Conwy's history as we explore fifty of its most iconic buildings. Some of these are well-known – indeed, world famous – others perhaps not so well-known, though each represents a stage or event in the history of Conwy and its hinterland, and its place in the wider world.

Above: Conwy Castle *c.* 1900, with the town and port nestling behind; Bodlondeb is on the rise beyond. Stephenson's tubular bridge crossing the river, in the distance the Great Orme.

Below: The view north-east from Caer Seion atop Conwy Mountain. First the A55, above that Conwy Marina, the River Conwy, Deganwy with the two hills of the Vadre, the Little Orme – to the upper left, Llandudno.

The 50 Buildings

1. Lletty'r Filiast, Great Orme, Llandudno

The Neolithic reached north Wales around 3500 BC and lasted approximately 1,500 years. A new way of life had developed thousands of miles away, its genesis focussed on the Middle East around 9000 BC. This was probably a reaction to climatic conditions becoming warmer and drier, leading to the first primitive crop-growing and stock-rearing, and the first permanent settlements. We became farmers, tending our herds and fields, though hunting continued to provide for a significant source of food. Other natural resources such as wood, bones, antlers and stone – especially flint – were utilised for making tools and weapons, as had been the case for many millennia.

For the early Neolithic there is evidence of close links with Ireland; indeed, research has emphasised the role of the western maritime routes and connections from Brittany to the western coast of Scotland. There seems to have been a fairly brief time during the

Lletty'r Filiast with donkeys, a species that arrived on these shores with the Romans. *Inset*: Neolithic hand axe from the Graig Lwyd 'axe factory' above Penmaenmawr. Examples of these have been found all over Britain. (Courtesy of Penmaenmawr Museum)

opening centuries of this period for large dwellings, often referred to as 'halls', being used in parts of Britain. It has been suggested that pioneering farming groups lived together in them until they felt sufficiently well-established in their new environment to separate into independent, smaller household groups. By the later Neolithic, people generally lived in isolated farms or small settlements. Allied with this change in settlement patterns there seems to have been a reorientation away from the western seaways towards the south and east, suggesting more traffic along this route.

Houses for the living tended to be made of wood, and it is only in ideal conditions of preservation that evidence remains for these. What has survived in north Wales, being constructed from massive stones, are their houses for the dead, in particular, cairns. These were not only repositories for the dead, they also symbolised permanence and continuity in the landscape and may have acted as boundary markers: 'This is our land; our ancestors have been buried here for generations.' Another social trend witnessed a change from communal tombs (portal dolmens) to individual graves furnished with goods and possessions indicating the person's social standing. Henges – circular earthworks with a bank and ditch used for ceremonial purposes – also appeared around this time, Stonehenge in Wiltshire being the prime example.

Close to the Bronze Age copper mines on the Great Orme stands Lletty'r Filiast, probably a portal dolmen, dating to between 3000 and 2000 BC. Its name in English means 'the lair of the greyhound bitch', although the reason for this is unknown. For its type it is quite small, measuring 2 metres by 1.6 metres and 1.25 metres high. It lies at the east end of a long oval mound comprising a natural outcrop of rock and the remains of the cairn which once would have covered it. The grave was robbed a long time ago and the only recorded finds have been a small piece of pottery and a bone.

2. Barclodiad y Gawres ('The Giantess's Apronful'), Bwlch y Ddeufaen, Rowen

Compared to the Neolithic period, the Bronze Age (2000 to 600 BC) is far better represented on the ground in our area. Furthermore, Bronze Age monuments are found on higher ground. Three possible causes have been suggested for this: exhaustion of soils in the lowlands after 1,000 or more years of agriculture; an increase in population; an improvement in the climate allowing higher ground to be exploited. A similarity between the two periods is the continuation of long-distance trade, although bronze artefacts, which conferred high status on their owners, were traded even further afield.

This trading promoted enterprises that can only be described as industrial ventures. One was the Bronze Age copper mines on the Great Orme. It began with surface mining in around 1600 BC, though towards the end of the Bronze Age deep underground galleries were opened up. While the full extent of the mining operation is unknown it is thought that it exceeds 24,000 square metres, incorporating more than 5 kilometres of passages to a depth of 70 metres. It has been estimated that no less than 1,800 tonnes of copper was extracted; given the narrowness of some of the tunnels it seems possible that children were employed as miners. Unfortunately there is little information about the mining communities.

It is likely that this copper travelled far from its source; indeed, it is thought that supply might have outstripped domestic demand, and international trade would have been the

Above: Bwlch y Ddeufaen. Standing stones either side of the ancient trackway; beyond the furthest stone lies Barclodiad y Gawres.

Below: Barclodiad y Gawres.

main outlet for the product. These Bronze Age communities were quite prosperous, sharing fashions of pottery and personal adornment with Ireland, Scotland and the rich trading centres of southern England.

In contrast to Neolithic burial traditions, Bronze Age burial monuments are round stone cairns or earthen barrows, built in prominent places such as ridges or along trackways. However, the earlier customs are largely maintained as each mound often covers a number of burials. A break with the Neolithic can be detected by the number of stone circles then being erected (for example, Druids' Circle above Penmaenmawr). Given the hours needed for their construction, these structures within a ceremonial landscape must have played a major role in the lives of these people.

Bwlch y Ddeufaen is a wide pass between the mountains at the west end of Rowen Valley. An ancient trackway runs along it, dotted on either side with many and varied monuments from both the Neolithic and Bronze Ages. The track is marked by two large standing stones, 2 metres and 3 metres high, though the age of these is uncertain. Lying a short distance east of the smaller stone is a large cairn, Barclodiad y Gawres. Its stones have been disturbed and it was stripped of grave goods a long time ago. It presents as an irregular oval, some 20 metres long, 13.5 metres wide and 1.2 metres high. A cist, a very large stone grave that should normally be at the centre, lies exposed on the north side. A bank of turf-covered stones lies on the southern edge.

By around 1600 BC people's beliefs appear to be changing, with the dead now being cremated and the ashes placed into a vessel for burial. After 1200 BC the climate deteriorated and settlements on the fragile soils of the upland were abandoned, with larger enclosed sites being established. A number of hillforts previously thought as being from the Iron Age are now dated earlier; an evolution from Bronze Age palisades to massive ramparts in the next period can be identified in north Wales. Weapons also became more common and warfare, possibly a consequence of diminishing territories, began to play a greater role.

3. Castell Caer Seion, Conwy Mountain

The standard history suggests that the Celts arrived in Wales in two waves. The first, the Hallstatt culture or 'Lowland Celts', originating from the region of the Danube in 1200 BC, reached here in around 600 BC and integrated peacefully with existing populations. The second wave, the 'True Celts' of the La Tène culture, originated in the mountainous regions of the Balkans and were warlike, governed by a patriarchal military aristocracy. They had settled in northern Italy by 400 BC, sacking Rome in 390 BC. There is an implication of mass migrations of Celts to Britain, annihilating local populations; it is more likely that a fierce elite lorded it over the indigenous peoples, as with the Normans in England over 1,000 years later.

Hill forts are traditionally associated with these warlike Celts. Caer Seion, majestically positioned atop Conwy Mountain, is one such fortification. It is believed to have been first occupied in around 300 BC and had two periods of building. In the first period, a single stone wall up to 4 metres deep encircled the whole hilltop, except at the sea-facing north side, with a single entrance on the south side. Within lay a village of over fifty roundhouses, the largest around 8 metres in diameter. The second period saw a smaller, stronger fort built at the west end; there was no access between the two forts. Other roundhouses

Above: Caer Seion: foundations of an Iron Age circular hut.

Below: Entrance to the inner fort. The Conwy Valley beyond, with the mountains of Snowdonia to the right.

have been identified lying outside the walls of both forts. Excavations in 1951 discovered over 400 sling stones near the entrance of the older fort. It may be that the smaller, better defended fort dates from AD 60–78, when Wales was under attack by the Romans. An absence of Roman finds could indicate that the fort was not occupied thereafter.

While Caer Seion and the other hill forts of north Wales stand proudly on lofty peaks, they are mute as to who exactly built and occupied them. More recent evidence proposes a very different history for the Celts: indeed, some would claim that grouping disparate Iron Age tribes under one label is inaccurate, and that there were no Celts – the 'Celtic World' being an invention of the eighteenth century. The notion of large-scale invasions and migrations has also been widely discredited. It cannot be denied that important cultural similarities can be identified across continental Europe and Britain, though these are more likely to be due to trade and similar contacts. The majority of the population of Wales during the Iron Age was probably of the same stock as in the preceding Bronze Age, who themselves descended largely from Britain's indigenous Neolithic and Mesolithic populations.

An even more startling claim has been made regarding the languages spoken by these peoples: evidence suggests that the Celtic languages evolved along the Atlantic seaways, and not in central Europe. Furthermore, DNA evidence is beginning to show that the groups who we now call the Celts originated on the north-west fringes of Europe and migrated east around 2000 BC, only to sweep back westwards again some 1,500 years later.

4. Canovium Roman Fort and St Mary's Church, Caerhun

In AD 43, Britain's cultural focus shifted dramatically as it became an outlying province of a vast empire centred firmly on an Italian coastal city – Rome. Over the next few decades most of Britain succumbed to the Roman legions, though they had a particular problem with the Druids, especially on Anglesey; the island was invaded twice, in AD 61 and AD 78. With the defeat of the Druids, the Roman way of life quickly spread across north Wales, and forts were constructed at Caernarfon (Segontium – the main Roman base in north

Canovium Roman fort, remains of the perimeter wall running left from St Mary's Church. (© Karen Alexander)

Above: Artist's impression of the fort in its heyday, bathhouse in foreground. (© Dave Alexander)

Below: St Mary's Church.

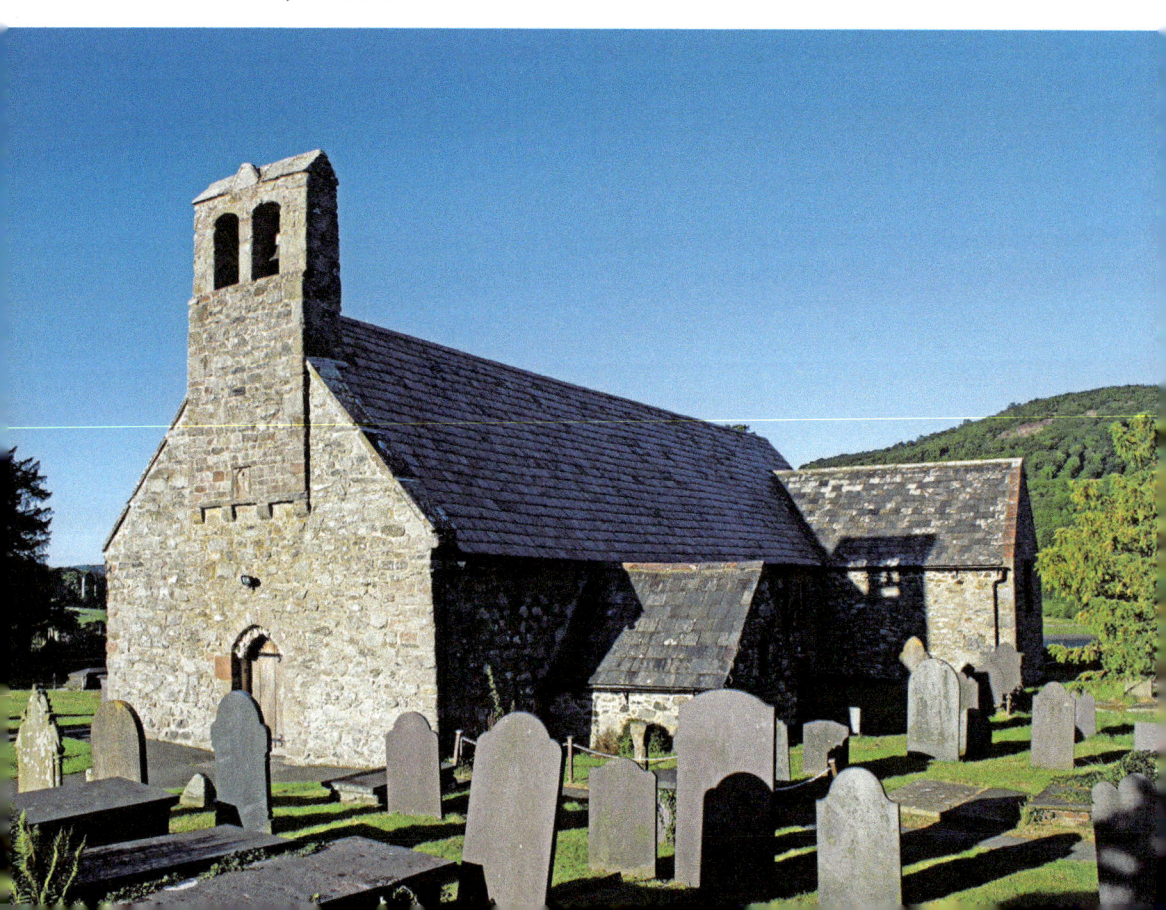

Wales), and down the Conwy valley at Caerhun (Canovium). Gwynedd, it seems, had to be closely monitored during these early decades.

Canovium was built during Agricola's campaign of AD 77–78 at a strategic crossing on the west bank of the River Conwy where the river ceased to be tidal. From Canovium the Roman road runs west to Segontium following the line of trackways used since Neolithic times, roughly north-west through Rowen to nearby Abergwyngregyn, thereafter following the coast to Segontium. Eastward, across the river at Tal-y-Cafn, the road leads to the great legionary centre and fortress of Castra Deva (Chester).

Canovium's first defences were a clay and rubble rampart, and timber buildings that housed 500 or so infantry and cavalrymen. In the middle of the second century the defences were rebuilt in stone. The fort's military function probably reduced steadily; civilian occupation continued into at least the fifth century. No extant buildings remain from the Roman period, although the outline of the fort can still be traced on the ground.

The Grade I-listed St Mary's Church was built in the north-eastern corner of the fort and dates in part from the thirteenth century. The squared, red sandstone blocks used in its construction possibly came from the fort. The small square-shaped stone built into the west wall, showing Christ crucified, dates to the 1400s; inside the church, the plain bowl font is medieval in origin. The church was altered and added to in the fifteenth and sixteenth centuries. The Gothic furnishings, simple pews with moulded rails to flat bench ends, date from around 1830. It lies in a quite delightful setting.

5. St Tudno's Church, Great Orme, Llandudno

There are many stories that tell of marvellous adventures and humble religious service connected with the earliest church in Wales, a period often referred to as the Age of the Saints. Many surviving place names tell of their founding saints; St Tudno is one of these.

St Tudno is reputed to have been the seventh son of Seithenyn, known as 'the Drunkard', who ruled sometime between AD 500–50 over Cantre'r Gwaelod, and whose wickedness and drunken folly caused the land to vanish beneath the inundating waters of Cardigan Bay. St Tudno's travels took him to the Great Orme where he found solace in a small cave. From here he took the message of Christianity to the few who lived on this windswept headland. A church was subsequently built and dedicated to him, hence Llandudno.

A tale similar in nature and date relates to the coast offshore from Penmaenmawr; here another wicked royal, Helig ap Glannog, tortured and murdered captured peasants for fun, until he too was punished by the sea when a mighty wave destroyed his palace, drowning all except the peasants who escaped to the clifftops. St Peris, one of his many sons, became a cardinal of Rome, who later retired to solitude in the mountains of north Wales: Llanberis is named after him. In these legends a common theme is that of a powerful but terrible father-king incurring watery retribution, whose sons were induced to embrace a hermitic way of life. Wickedness invoking a watery extinction, leaving survivors who seek the Faith, somewhat mirrors the Biblical story of Noah and his Ark.

Centuries earlier the Roman Empire adopted Christianity as the state religion, and by AD 375 it was the empire's leading faith. As Rome's power diminished over the next centuries, and continental Europe descended into interminable civil wars and barbarian pressure from the east, the western seaways of Europe took on a greater and renewed

St Tudno's Church. The outdoor pulpit was added in 1912.

significance. Along this route travelled missionaries preaching and converting – the Celtic saints. Ireland, never under Roman rule so able to develop its own ideas after conversion by St Patrick, was a vigorous source of this religious energy, as evidenced by the number of ogham (early Irish language) inscriptions on stones found in lands around the Irish Sea. Perhaps it is in these waters that the story of St Tudno's arrival on the Great Orme should be anchored.

Whatever the legends or surmised history tell us, the present St Tudno's Church lies in a spectacular setting in a hollow facing the Irish Sea. Rectangular in shape, it comprises a nave and a chancel with no structural division, and a small north porch and vestry. The earliest part, the north wall of the nave, dates to the 1100s or early 1200s. The south wall and the west gable wall with its small doorway were rebuilt in the 1400s, the chancel and north porch being added sometime later. The bell turret and the vestry are modern. The font dates to the late twelfth or early thirteenth century – in the nineteenth century it was taken outside and used as a trough. Two grave slabs from the 1200s were built into the south wall of the nave. In 1839, a storm ripped off the roof, and it was only sixteen years later that it was restored and reopened, and the font returned to its rightful place. It was reported that the church retained many frescos, mainly coloured red. By this time the new town of Llandudno was on its way to being a major tourist destination. The little church continues to be used for services, held outside on fine Sundays during the summer months, and also hosts concerts.

6. Deganwy Castle, The Vardre, Deganwy

Throughout Europe, regimes led by a local 'Big Man' emerged wherever Rome's central authority disintegrated. With the final Roman withdrawal from Britain in AD 410, petty kingdoms sprang up; not just in Wales, but further east in what was becoming the land of Angles and Saxons. Inevitably, these kingdoms were soon at war with their neighbours: in Wales that meant fellow Welsh, Mercians, or seaborne Irish. A further casualty of Rome's departure was advanced military and civil engineering, and buildings were once again made largely of wood leaving no archaeological record.

The narrative for the immediate post-Roman period abounds with legends, traditions and folk tales – King Arthur, perhaps, being the most well known of these – but little recorded history. The first attested individual in north Wales is Maelgwyn, King of Gwynedd (d. approximately AD 549). He was praised fulsomely by bards and was unusually learned for a king of his time, actively supporting the work of the Welsh Church by setting aside land upon which churches were founded. A general 'good sort' it would appear, though his contemporary Gildas was of the opinion that he was a drunken tyrant. Maelgwyn's court and political centre was based in Deganwy, on the hill behind the current village. Excavations carried out in 1961 confirmed occupation during this period; finds included amphorae which had once held imported wine, but no buildings were located. Maelgwyn's dynasty came to an end in AD 825; records tell of the castle's destruction by invading Mercians in AD 822.

Deganwy Castle, probably 1215 or later, with the Great Orme in the background. *Inset*: Statue showing an idealised representation of Llewelyn the Great standing proudly in Lancaster Square, Conwy: by E. O. Griffith, Liverpool, 1895.

Deganwy Castle, 1245–54.

The site appears next in history in 1080, when the Norman adventurer Robert of Rhuddlan built a castle here. However, his attempted conquest of north Wales failed and the castle was regained by the Welsh. The building was praised by Giraldus Cambrensis in 1191; unfortunately it was not long before it was again razed to the ground, this time to stop it falling into the hands of King John (1199–1216).

By 1213 the area had returned to Welsh control, and Llewelyn ap Iorwerth (the Great) built another castle on the site. Some vestiges of this remain and a fine corbel has been excavated, probably a representation of the king. However, in 1240, Llewelyn's sons and heirs felt too weak to resist Henry III's advancing army and demolished the castle: when the English camped on the site in 1245 it is said that they had to sleep in tents. Henry set about rebuilding the castle, which continued up to 1254, but was never completed – though the town, by then nestling on the shoreline beneath the hills, had been granted its charter. It changed hands again in 1263 when it was taken by Llewelyn ap Gruffudd after a long siege. As others had before him, he set about demolishing it. It was now effectively abandoned, and it is these remains that are most evident today.

This brief chronicle of Deganwy Castle tells of a strategic border location constantly changing hands as invasion and reconquest ebbed and flowed over the centuries. Perhaps the biggest irony for the castle is that it has been suggested that stone from it was used to build the castle of north Wales' final invader, that of Edward I in Conwy.

7. Llys Euryn, Rhos on Sea, Colwyn Bay

On driving into Colwyn Bay from the west along the A55, a rounded hill rises above the surrounding housing. This is Bryn Euryn. It does not seem to be a remarkable feature of the landscape, yet it has direct links to Welsh princes and to Henry VII, the first of the Tudor dynasty.

Llys Euryn.

The summit awaits excavation, but it is thought that an Iron Age hillfort, which remained in use until the early Middle Ages, lies there. Its visible remains show a strongly defended inner wall and a less substantial outer wall, reminiscent of defensive sites of the sixth century. The medieval name for this area was Dinerth – 'the fort of the bear'. Gildas, writing sometime before AD 545, mentions Cynlas Goch, king of Rhos, a cousin of Maelgwyn whose court lay at Deganwy: Cynlas was described by Gildas as belonging to the 'bear's refuge'.

The ruins of Llys Euryn lie not on the hill's summit but lower down; in the early 1200s it was home to Ednyfed Fychan (d. 1246). He came from a family well established in the royal court of the princes of Gwynedd. Ednyfed gave military and political service to Llewelyn the Great, for which he was granted much land. His descendants continued the family tradition of holding offices in high places and with their widespread land possessions, enjoyed considerable wealth. They became the forerunners of the Welsh squires whose emergence is characteristic of the period following the conquests of Edward I.

One of Ednyfed's sons, Tudur, was captured during Henry III's inconclusive campaign in September 1245, though he was released in May 1247 on swearing fealty to the king of England. Three brothers, Goronwy, Rhys and Gwilym, were in the personal following of Richard II (1377–99), but joined the revolt of Owain Glyndwr after Richard had been dethroned in 1399. The revolt began in 1400 but, after initial successes, it was put down by 1412. A fourth brother, Maredudd, who somehow escaped all this, was the father of Owain Tudur and great-grandfather of Henry VII (1485–1509). The journey from Bryn Euryn has thus led us directly to Bosworth Field in 1485, and indirectly to a Leicester car park in 2012 where the resting place of Richard III, the loser of this battle, was discovered.

After the Glyndwr uprising, most of the family's lands were forfeited to the Crown and came into the possession of the Gruffudds of Penrhyn, themselves descendants of Ednyfed Fychan: another important local family, the Mostyns, also claim descent from Ednyfed. The visible remains of Llys Euryn date from later in the 1400s, when the house was rebuilt by Robin ap Gruffudd Coch. Descendants of Robin's heir, Huw Conwy (who also fought with Henry VII), made alterations to the building. This family initially prospered, though fell out of favour around the time of the Reformation, probably due to their Catholic sympathies. They went bankrupt in the early 1600s but some family members remained as tenants until 1654. The old house may have continued to have residents into the 1700s, then it fell into disrepair.

8. St Mary's Church, Conwy

Up to the twelfth century the political focus of the region was on the opposite side of the river, at Deganwy. On the Aberconwy side stood the religious centre; a Cistercian monastery was established in around 1192 and St Mary's was originally the abbey church. The monastery quickly became the leading religious house in north Wales, enjoying the patronage of the Welsh princes and their families; it also became the burial place of a number of them, including Llewelyn the Great in 1240. Five years later marauding English soldiers under Henry III plundered the abbey, removing chalices and books and committing sundry other damage; it suffered further harm in 1283 during Edward I's conquest. After Edward moved the monastery south to Maenan to make room for his castle and new town, St Mary's became the parish church. Llewelyn's coffin was also moved to Maenan; empty and lidless, it is now traditionally held to reside in Llanrwst Church.

Although little archaeology survives of the period before Edward, the churchyard may hold clues to the abbey precinct's boundary, enclosed and bounded as it is by the high walls and gardens of Rose Hill Street, Church Street, High Street and Castle Street. It has been suggested that this block of land reflects the precinct of the Cistercian abbey as it interrupts the regular system of streets laid out at the town's foundation.

Little masonry of the original church building survives; it was extensively rebuilt and altered in the 1300s and the following two centuries. In 1872, it was systematically restored with further work after 1878 and during the early 1920s. Internally the church has many noteworthy details: for example, a fine carved rood screen separating the chancel from the nave dates to around 1497–1501. An effigy in the south aisle is purportedly of Mary Williams (d. 1585), mother of John Williams, Archbishop of York during the reign of Charles I, though a recent suggestion is that this attribution is unlikely as the style of clothing dates from an earlier period. In the chancel lies a sandstone tomb-chest of Robert Wynn (d. 1598), the builder of Plas Mawr, along with a floor slab from 1637 inscribed 'Nicholas Hookes': he is described as the forty-first child of his father, William Hookes, who apparently, apart from being married, had rather a lot of 'friends'. Nicholas himself went on to father only twenty-seven children.

For around thirty-five years the church has been the venue for the Conwy Classical Music Festival, where, in the first week of the school summer holidays, lunchtime and evening concerts can be enjoyed in this ancient building.

Above: St Mary's Church.

Below left: Font, probably late 1400s.

Below right: Effigy in the south aisle, purportedly of Mary Williams (d. 1585).

9. Conwy Castle

For centuries north Wales had endured raiding parties and invasions from the east, including Mercians, Normans, and by the 1200s, a more determined foe: Plantagenet English kings. Both John (1199–1216) and Henry III (1216–72) had attempted to subdue the Welsh princes militarily and by the gentler means of arranged dynastic marriages. However, apart from some short-term gains, they were unsuccessful in their efforts. In 1267, circumstances forced Henry to negotiate a peace, the Treaty of Montgomery, which saw Llewelyn ap Gruffudd not only affirming his position in north Wales but extending his territories into mid-Wales and England. Henry had to recognise Llewelyn as Prince of Wales, the overlord of all other Welsh princes; in return, Llewelyn had to acknowledge Henry as his own overlord. And so the seeds of conflict were sown.

Edward I (b. 1239, reigned 1272–1307) learned of the death of his father, Henry III, while returning from the Ninth Crusade. Ambitious and a 'man of action', he was soon enforcing his will on his neighbours and could presume to receive homage from Llewelyn – which he refused to do in 1273. Llewelyn also refused to pay the annual dues he had agreed to with the Treaty of Montgomery. To compound matters, in 1264 Llewelyn had become betrothed to Eleanor de Montfort, and in 1275 the decision was taken to get married. This was an outrageous political move against Edward since Eleanor was the daughter of Simon de Montfort, who had led the Barons' Revolt against Edward's father (and Eleanor's uncle), Henry III, during which Llewelyn had sided with de Montfort. During de Montfort's last battle, at Evesham in 1265, a twelve-man hit squad of Edward's men sought him out with the aim of killing him, which they achieved quite gruesomely. Edward was ruthless, as time would tell.

Eleanor was captured by Edward in 1275 as she was voyaging to England from France for her wedding; she spent the next three years in prison at Windsor. In 1276 her husband-to-be was declared a rebel after failing to pay homage for a third time and Edward led a brutal campaign into north Wales, largely financed by a severe taxation he had made on the Jewish community in 1275. Edward's strategy was to force Llewelyn back into the stronghold of Gwynedd. Although this was accomplished, Llewelyn was never defeated in battle, but his position was so weakened that in the Treaty of Aberconwy of 1277 Edward became overlord of all Welsh princes; displacing Llewelyn, who lost his previous gains including all territory east of the River Conwy.

However, all this did not prevent Edward from giving his cousin Eleanor de Montfort away at her wedding to Llewelyn in Worcester Cathedral in 1278. Edward paid for the wedding festivities, but politics were still close at hand as Llewelyn was encouraged – under duress according to him – to reaffirm past treaties. Eleanor died at Llewelyn's royal palace at Abergwyngregyn in 1282, the year that Dafydd, Llewelyn's younger brother, stormed Hawarden Castle, initiating rebellion against Edward. Llewelyn, perhaps reluctantly, joined his brother's enterprise, but after initial successes he was killed near Builth in December. Dafydd assumed the title Prince of Wales, but his situation was untenable and in June 1283 he was captured and executed. The age of Welsh princes was over.

To cement his victory Edward immediately set about building those imperious symbols of power, the four great castles of north Wales: Harlech, Caernarfon, Beaumaris and Conwy. They were the most ambitious and concentrated building projects of medieval Europe. Conwy Castle required vast sums and an army of workmen (at its peak 1,500 were employed), supervised by

Conwy Castle: the four towers in the foreground enclose the inner ward, which contained the royal apartments. (© Crown copyright (2016) Welsh Government)

Above: Conwy Castle from the east. (© Crown copyright (2016) Welsh Government) *Inset*: Contemporary silver penny of Edward I showing his (stylised) facing portrait.

Below: The outer ward looking west towards the gatehouse, with the curving great hall on the left. (© Crown copyright (2016) Welsh Government)

specialists such as the master military architect of his age, James of St George. They were the final development of the crusader castles, which Edward had seen in the Holy Land.

There were perhaps two reasons why Edward chose to build his castle on the site of Aberconwy monastery rather than on the ancient site of Deganwy. The first was symbolic, usurping not only military and political power but also matters spiritual: furthermore, it was the burial place of Llewelyn the Great. The second was more prosaic: to establish a new and economically viable town, one more easily defended and better placed for receiving supplies by sea. The castle was almost completed by 1287, but Edward spent only a brief time there. In December 1294, while attempting to defeat the rebellion under Madog ap Llewelyn, he was cut off from his main forces by floods and was obliged to seek shelter and safety in the castle. A month later the floods had subsided and he was able to cross the river and put the rebels to flight.

By the 1320s the fortunes of Conwy Castle were in decline. Various attempts were made over the next few decades to restore it, but by the 1390s it was again in decay. It was under these conditions that Richard II sought refuge there from Henry Bolingbroke, though he eventually surrendered; he was murdered at Pontefract, and Bolingbroke was crowned Henry IV. Two years later the castle was taken by supporters of Owain Glyndwr, who held it for three months.

Its garrison was strengthened during the Wars of the Roses (1455–85), and during the reign of Henry VIII the castle and town walls were extensively repaired. Royal ownership of the castle ended in 1627 when it was sold for £100 to Edward, first Baron Conwy. It saw action again in the Civil War. However, the technology of war was advancing and gunpowder was soon to make castles such as this outmoded; it was considered to be suitable only as an artillery emplacement and for the detention of prisoners. By 1665, Lord Conwy had no further use for his castle and set about dismantling it, salvaging the castle's ironwork and lead from the roof. Fortunately for posterity, the castle survived far better than most of the period, and today it remains Conwy's most iconic building.

10. Conwy Town Walls

Edward I was the king of England from 1272 to 1307. He was also the Duke of Gascony in south-west France. His great-grandfather, Henry, married Duchess Eleanor of Aquitaine in 1152 after her divorce from Louis VII of France and when, in 1154, Henry was crowned Henry II of England he also became the Duke of Aquitaine, a vast tract of land in south-west France. Though the extent diminished as the decades passed, English kings held this territory until defeat at the end of the Hundred Years War in 1453.

Edward may have been the English king, but he spoke little or no English. Since the Norman Conquest the language of court had been French; and of the Church, Latin. It was only after the start of the Hundred Years War in 1337 that speaking French in England became somewhat suspect (were they French spies?), and English kings became bilingual in French and English. The first king of England to use English as his first language was Henry IV (1399–1413); for centuries only the lower orders spoke English. So, if Edward thought that English was beneath him, we can only guess at his opinion of the Welsh language.

For most of the 1200s *bastides* – fortified new towns – had been built in Gascony, and the Duke of Gascony's concept for his new borough of Conwy was heavily influenced by

View from Tower 13 along the town wall towards the river, with the town to the right and Town Ditch Road to the left. (© Crown copyright (2016) Welsh Government)

Above: Upper Gate, main landward gate into Conwy. (© Crown copyright (2016) Welsh Government)

Below: Lying between Towers 15 and 16 are the only windows in the entire circuit of the walls, probably marking the site of 'Llewelyn's Hall'.

this form of town planning. Conwy was not conceived simply as a castle: it was part of a whole which included the town, both reliant on each other for protection and trade. Once built, Conwy would have been populated by migrants from England, and English and French would have been spoken – it is possible that those from Gascony and Savoy who had built the castle and town walls settled in Conwy. However, it has been estimated that by around 1300, 8 per cent of the town's inhabitants were native Welsh. It would take another 200 years before a poet, Huw Bulkeley, could write of Conwy: '*Y dre a'r wlad/ yn ordr lân/Yn un laith a wnanwn weithian*.' (We now make the town and the country one language/people in good order.)

The new town's walls run for 1,400 yards and enclose an area, roughly triangular in shape, of around 22 acres. One side lies along the quay and has a projecting wall running down into the water at the end furthest from the castle, offering further protection. Twenty-one towers punctuate the wall at regular intervals; three twin-towered gates allowed access into the town. A surrounding ditch completed the defences. Conwy would have been an imposing sight to contemporaries – that being, of course, Edward's intention.

11. St Benedict's Church, Henrhyd Road, Gyffin

Gyffin Church occupies an interesting location. It lies next to a river, may originally have had a circular churchyard, and though very close to the estuary of the River Conwy, it hides behind a ridge, tucked out of the sight of pirates and other seaborne miscreants. This

St Benedict's Church.

Three of the sixteen panels depicting saints.

situation is reminiscent of early Celtic churches, bringing to mind St David's Cathedral which also sits next to a river and, though close to the sea, is not visible from it. Did an earlier wooden building stand on this site? Was Gyffin Church once dedicated to a Celtic saint? Was it rededicated sometime in that turbulent century between the founding of Aberconwy monastery and Edward I's settlement? All these questions are, of course, pure conjecture as there is no evidence to support any answers. Allowing for this, it remains intriguing to speculate whether a church stood here in AD 880 when Anarawd, prince of north Wales, defeated in battle Edred, Earl of Mercia, at nearby Cymryd.

It is assumed that Gyffin Church was founded sometime in the 1200s by monks from nearby Aberconwy monastery – the font dates from this time. The earliest physical evidence shows that the chancel and the extended nave date to the 1400s. Perhaps the church's most noteworthy highlight is the curved chancel ceiling, featuring sixteen painted panels depicting saints dating from the fifteenth century. These full-length figures, in red, olive and grey against a foliage background, are now a little faded, but are important as the only coherent church paintings in Gwynedd from this period.

12. Aberconwy House, High Street, Conwy

Tree-ring dating has shown that timbers from different storeys in Aberconwy House were taken from trees felled from 1417–20; this makes Aberconwy House the earliest securely dated secular domestic building in Wales. It stands on three floors, the lower two and the south gable having stone rubble walls while the upper is of timber construction with jetties, unusually on two sides, likely indicating that the builder was originally from the West Midlands or Cheshire. Jettying was a method for increasing the interior space; it also indicated that the owner was wealthy. The upper two floors were living quarters, the basement a shop or store. This ground floor, now around a metre below the level of the road outside, was entered through a door on the street corner; this is now a window, the present door having been built in the seventeenth century. The outside stairs are a relatively new addition, a response to the rising road level. As may be expected given its age, the building has been modified a number of times over the centuries.

The location of Aberconwy House suggests that it was built for a merchant of some standing. It occupies the corner plot of two principal streets and lies directly opposite Porth Isaf, the main gate through the town walls from the quay – a prime situation in a town built on maritime trade. It might be inferred that a wealthy merchant could only operate in a town that was successful in its endeavours and that Conwy was carving out a position as the prime location on the north Wales coast. Indeed, contemporary poet Ieuan ap Gruffudd Leiaf celebrated the beer of Conwy in verse, though this was mainly an expression of the variety of different Welsh beers available in a port town.

The first named individual connected with Aberconwy House is Evan David, a trader who died in 1663. He held plots of land to the south of the town and would bring the produce to his shop to sell. The commodities traded had changed by the early nineteenth century when merchant-mariner Captain Samuel Williams held the premises, dealing in lead, copper and slate. By the middle of the century it had become a temperance hotel – proprietor Mr E. Richardson, may have been slightly optimistic in 1857 when he advertised that the hotel was 'only a two minute walk' from the railway station. We do not know what thoughts he might have had about Ieuan's poem. Mr William Jones held the hotel a year later and a coffee shop was opened. At the visit from the Duke and Duchess of

A busy Castle Street in front of Aberconwy House *c.* 1880.

Aberconwy House.

York to Conwy in May 1899, the 'Aberconway' Temperance Hotel 'floated their own pennant' as part of a fully bedecked town's decorations. By then the old building was a known landmark of distinction and it could be reported that, 'it is worth noting that the Aberconway is full of antiquarian interest from the fact that its quaint coffee-room was built so long ago as the year 1400.'

It was a museum and an antique shop by around 1910. In 1934 Mr Alexander Campbell Blair gave the building to the National Trust, thus foiling a plan to dismantle the house and cart it off to the United States. Today, it continues to be one of the treasures of the National Trust.

13. No. 11 Castle Street, Conwy (former Black Lion Inn)

Probably constructed as a two-bay hall, this is the second oldest of two medieval buildings remaining in the town after nearby Aberconwy House; archaeological evidence taken from an original cruck (roof timber) suggests that the building was erected sometime after 1442. It was modified to a storeyed house and had a main chimney inserted in around 1589. This date above the door, along with the initials 'JB E', are believed to relate to John Brickdall,

No. 11 Castle Street, formerly the Black Lion inn.

the vicar of Conwy, and his wife Em, to commemorate the rebuilding of the house when they were living there. The bays and dormer windows at the front of the house were added later, and further alterations took place when the building was converted to an inn. In the *Whitehall Evening Post* in 1760, William and Jonat Evans informed the public that they had kept the Black Lion in Conwy from 1746–49, showing that it was actively an inn at this time – and possibly before then. Towards the mid-nineteenth century, markets were held at the Black Lion for wheat, barley, oats and beans, and it was the venue for public auctions of property within the district. An outbuilding at the back of the inn was also a local centre for pig-dealing until the end of the century.

In July 1897 the Black Lion, with fellow Conwy inns the Albion and the Erskine Arms, were subject to a draft conveyance (in consideration of £5,350) to Ind Coope & Co. Ltd. The brewery firm held on to the Black Lion until 1935, when they rebuilt the Blue Bell next door. To further stimulate trade in their new location they prohibited the sale of alcohol in the Black Lion, a clause that was to remain for all subsequent owners. From 1935 to the late 1970s various businesses were run from the building, including a teashop and antiques shop. In 2002 it was bought by the owner of a local car-repair business, who began a restoration. One of his panel beaters created the metal jackdaws that perch on the tops of the front dormers, reflecting the tradition that anybody born within Conwy's town walls is known as a 'jackdaw'. A private owner bought the building in 2008 and completed its renovation for residential use in 2015.

14. Gloddaeth Hall, Llandudno

The Mostyns are the oldest landowning family in Wales, after the Crown. The estate of Gloddaeth came to the family around 1460 when Margaret – the great-granddaughter of Madoc Gloddaeth – married Hywel ap Ieuan Fychan of Mostyn, in the present-day county of Flintshire.

The earliest part of the present building dates from at least the early sixteenth century, and possibly back to Margaret Mostyn's time. The Great Hall is both medieval and ancestral in design, despite being Tudor in date. The solar wing – also a traditional feature of a medieval manor house and used as the family's private living and sleeping area – dates from the same period. The listing text of Gloddaeth Hall – a Grade I-listed building – describes it as a 'large multi-period country house', and Pevsner's *Architectural Guide* mentions various extant additions and alterations from the sixteenth and seventeenth centuries. However, the late nineteenth century brought the biggest changes to the house.

In 1855, Lady Henrietta Augusta Nevill – the daughter of a Kentish earl – married Thomas Mostyn, the heir apparent to the second Baron Mostyn. Thomas died of consumption just six years later, at the tragically early age of thirty-one, leaving the widowed Lady Augusta with two small sons. She also faced having to save the inheritance of her elder son from complex family indebtedness. The second baron, Edward Lloyd-Mostyn, had obtained the Enclosure Act in 1848, which enabled the creation of Llandudno as a fashionable seaside resort. However, despite Llandudno's continuing development, the scale of the family's debts was becoming a severe problem. Lady Augusta staunchly resisted suggestions that family lands be sold off, insisting that selling Llandudno would be disadvantageous to her son's interests.

The sixteenth-century hall.

It was also under the stewardship of Lady Augusta that Gloddaeth Hall had two major alterations: the first, in 1876, involved substantial changes to the Lower End, while the second saw an entire new range added to the west side in 1889, almost doubling the size of the house. Lady Augusta oversaw the renovations at Bodysgallen, the other Mostyn house close to Gloddaeth, around the same time. She returned to live at Gloddaeth Hall in 1879 until her death in 1912, having dedicated her life to contributing to the development of Llandudno and district; the significance of her role as a benefactor to the town is difficult to overestimate.

In 1935, after a sale of contents, the estate let the house and parkland as Gloddaeth School for Girls, and from 1965 as St David's College, a co-educational independent school, still housed there today.

15. Penrhyn Old Hall, Penrhyn Bay

Although surviving today as a mostly Tudor manor house, parts of Penrhyn Old Hall could date back even further. The Penrhyn family is mentioned in records dating from the reign of Edward III (1327–77), and the building was described as an 'ancient stone house' in the 1549 itinerary of Henry VIII's antiquary, John Leyland. It was evidently an important place during Elizabethan times: the cartographer Christopher Saxton included it in his mapping of the district in 1575, but excluded the great houses of Gloddaeth and Bodysgallen, also known to have been in existence at the time.

Penrhyn Old Hall.

Dating mainly from around 1550, the south-west wing is the oldest section of the house. Its Baronial Hall has a carving above the fireplace with a symbol of Christianity, indicating that the elements of Eucharist were kept at the house. The room above is heavily beamed and trussed; an even earlier wattle-and-daub wall is decorated with sixteenth-century frescos, which were whitewashed over and only rediscovered during renovations in 1910.

The north-east wing, originally a separate building, dates from around 1590 when it was occupied by the Pughs, a powerful Roman Catholic family whose coat of arms is over the front doorway. In an age when Protestantism was the only religion allowed by the monarch and State these were dangerous times to be a Catholic, and the Pughs celebrated Mass secretly in the small chapel in the grounds. There is also a 'priest hole' with room for six men inside the large fireplace in the current Tudor Bar, where priests could hide if the house was searched. A stone dated 1590 above the fireplace commemorates Robert Pugh's domestic chaplain, William Davies. Tipped off in 1586 that recusants were on the verge of even greater persecution than before, Pugh and Davies fled to the Little Orme where they lived in the comparative safety of a cave for nearly a year, when they wrote a book together and managed to smuggle in a small printing press. The book was *Y Drych Gristianogawl* (The Christian Mirror), and is reputed to be the first book ever printed in Wales.

The men managed to escape in 1587 when their sanctuary was discovered, but were arrested five years later at Holyhead while trying to board a boat to Ireland. Robert Pugh evaded capture again, but Davies was incarcerated in the dungeons of Beaumaris Castle. He was convicted at assizes of being a Catholic priest and hanged, drawn and quartered on 27 July 1593, after which parts of his body were displayed, in the gory cautionary manner of the time, on the castle gateways at Beaumaris, Caernarfon and Conwy. He was beatified by the Pope in 1987.

Penrhyn stayed in the Pugh family until 1760 when it was sold by the last of the family line; it later passed to the Owen family, who found a hoard of Roman coins on the property in 1873. Another hoard was discovered in 1907 by Edward Booth-Jones, an antiques dealer who occupied the house until 1915 when he perished, along with his wife and two young children, in the tragic sinking, by a German U-boat, of the *Lusitania* as the family were returning from a business trip to America.

Following its use as a private house, Penrhyn became an antique shop and museum, a hotel, and tearooms. It was bought in 1963 by the Marsh family, by which time it was in a poor state of repair and required extensive restoration. It continues to be run by the Marshes today as a pub and restaurant.

16. Plas Mawr, High Street, Conwy

'That immense pile of building called Plas Mawr', as it was labelled in 1830, is not how we might define it nowadays, although we would agree with the additional sentiment that it 'is a property of very great value'.

The builder of this pile was Robert Wynn (1520–98), born at Gwydir Castle. He was the third son of John Wyn ap Maredudd, who inherited an estate based on Dolwyddelan Castle. John prospered and acquired much of the land of the former Cistercian abbey at Maenan after the Dissolution of the Monasteries. Robert, though, inherited very little and had to make his own fortune. In his mid-teens he entered the household of Philip Hoby, one of the gentlemen serving in the king's privy chamber. Exact details of Robert's role in Philip's household are not clear, but it may be safely assumed that he travelled widely in Britain and Europe with his master, visiting some of the more resplendent courts.

Robert appears in north Wales' records in the 1540s, when in his twenties. For the next twenty years he turned his hand to business, amassing a fortune through land rents and importing wine into Conwy from France. With no substantial estate of his own, Robert decided to base his household in Conwy, a fashionable gentlemen's residence at the time. In around 1570 he married Dorothy Griffith, a member of the local gentry. To provide for his new wife, Robert bought a mansion house for £200 with a garden and three orchards in Conwy, and built Plas Mawr there. Robert rose in local society, becoming a Justice of the Peace, MP for Caernarvonshire in 1589, and the county sheriff in 1590–91. Dorothy died childless in 1586; two years later, when in his seventies, Robert married a much younger lady, Dorothy Dymock, with whom he had seven children in six years. One is tempted to recall Nicholas Hookes' 1637 inscription in St Mary's Church and wonder whether there was something in Conwy's water. Robert died in 1598; his tomb-chest lies in St Mary's chancel.

Plas Mawr ('Great Hall') was built in three phases between 1576 and 1585, beginning with the rectangular north wing at the top of what is now Crown Lane, followed in 1580 by the central block facing the lane with matching south wing, forming a symmetrical courtyard house. It was not until 1585 that Robert was able to acquire the corner plot facing the High Street on which he built the gatehouse, thereby making a second courtyard. Despite being built in three phases the whole has a coherence, the north wing setting the

Above left: Gatehouse. (© Crown copyright (2016) Welsh Government)

Above right: The great chamber, the ceremonial focus of the Elizabethan household. (© Crown copyright (2016) Welsh Government) *Inset*: Profuse symbolism on the chimney breast of Robert's hall, including his initials, 'R-W'. (© Crown copyright (2016) Welsh Government)

Below: Upper terrace flower beds, planted with varieties popular in the 1600s. (© Crown copyright (2016) Welsh Government)

style for the later additions. Internally, the ornate plasterwork follows a fashion set by Henry VIII and adopted by the gentry and the mercantile class as a relatively inexpensive method of introducing colour and emblematic devices to Elizabethan houses; Plas Mawr is recognised as an early and almost complete survival of this type of decoration.

After Robert's death Plas Mawr passed to his wife, but a legal dispute over his will was not resolved until 1630 and there was no money to make alterations or improvements to the building; it is likely that this helped preserve Plas Mawr as it was. 1637 saw Robert's grandson, another Robert, inherit the house. A surviving inventory of 1664 has made it possible to refurnish Plas Mawr in an authentic manner and gives an indication of each room's function. In 1683, Robert's daughter Elin married Robert Wynne of Bodysgallen and Plas Mawr thus became part of his extensive estates; consequently, the house was not likely to have been lived in by the family. The Wynnes married into the Mostyn family and the present Lord Mostyn remains Plas Mawr's freeholder.

For the eighteenth and most of the nineteenth century Plas Mawr was subdivided and rented out for a number of purposes, including as a furniture and carpenter's shop, an infant school, and as tenements for various families. In a report of 1885, a plea was made for the Corporation to 'obtain possession of the place, and preserve it, from whitewash, dilapidation, etc' in order to 'arrest its decay'. Two years later the Royal Cambrian Academy of Art leased the building, undertaking to conserve and restore the structure and its decoration. The academy's members displayed works of art in the principal rooms; in 1993 they moved to new premises and Plas Mawr was placed into the care of Cadw, who began a four-year restoration programme. It opened to the public in 1997, winning the Building Conservation Award of the Royal Institute of Chartered Surveyors. Now this wonderful 'pile' welcomes visitors to the 'finest Elizabethan townhouse in Britain'.

17. The Old College, Castle Street, Conwy

When walking along Castle Street away from the castle, a building on the left informs us that this was 'Yr Hen Goleg – Ye Old College'. Illustrations from the early nineteenth century depict previous manifestations similarly describing it as The Old College. However it gained its name, the building sits firmly in the 'tradition would have it' mould. The earliest archaeological details date from around 1500, since when it has been subjected to many modifications and modernisations. Local historians are divided as to whether it ever functioned as a school. It has been suggested that Dr John Williams, with financial assistance from his relative Sir John Wynn of Gwydir, hoped to establish a school in Conwy, and perhaps this is that school.

John Williams was born in Aberconwy in 1582. He descended on his father's side from the houses of Cochwillan and Penrhyn, and on his mother's from the house of Wynn of Gwydir. Educated at Ruthin Grammar School and St John's College, Cambridge, he clearly came from a wealthy and well-connected family. By 1611 he was winning favour with James I (1603–25) and his career, both religious and lay, soon led him into the heart of the court. He rose to positions of power, becoming Dean of Westminster, Keeper of the Great Seal, and, by 1621, Bishop of Lincoln. During his career he endowed several libraries, including those of Westminster School and St John's College, Cambridge.

The Old College. *Inset*: Line engraving of John Williams, Bishop of Lincoln, *c.* 1621–25 (© National Portrait Gallery, London)

Unfortunately, James' successor Charles I (1625–49) did not think so highly of John and, in 1625, he was relieved of the Great Seal. Matters continued to worsen and in 1637 he was imprisoned in the Tower of London. He was released in 1640 and joined Charles at York, where he became archbishop in 1641. Later that year he was again in the Tower and on his release in 1642 he joined the king in Yorkshire, but soon headed back to north Wales – initially supporting the Royalist cause and basing himself in Conwy Castle, which he may have repaired and fortified at his own cost. His influence with the king was fading though; in May 1645 he was unceremoniously turned out of Conwy Castle by the Royalist commander. John soon realised that the king's cause was lost and, after negotiating with the local Parliamentarian commander, swapped sides and took an active part in the storming of Conwy in August 1646. After Charles I's execution in 1649, John appears to have been reconciled with the Royalist cause, as at his death on 25 March 1650 he was staying with the Mostyns of Gloddaeth – a Royalist house.

Does this help us determine whether John Williams was the founder of the Old College? Perhaps not. What it does display is that he was actively, and numerously, endowing libraries and other concerns and was able to finance the repair of Conwy Castle. That there was a school in Conwy in February 1645 is evidenced by a report that the bishop of St Asaph decided he could risk leaving his son there, even though the town was still 'in a ferment' with the Civil War going on around it. Evidently, John Williams prospered while living in 'interesting times' and had both the resources and the connections to set up a small school in his home town. But whether he did so is unknown, and moreover, if he had done so it was not necessarily at the site now named The Old College.

18. Bodysgallen Hall, Llandudno

Situated in over 200 acres around 1 mile south of Llandudno, Bodysgallen is a notable example of land and property in the area changing hands over the years between important local families through dynastic intermarriage – in Bodysgallen's case between the Wynns and the Mostyns, whose family seat of Gloddaeth lies only a short distance north of Bodysgallen.

The name may mean either 'house among thistles' or a corruption of 'the abode of Cadwallon', a king of Gwynedd who died in AD 517. Whether Cadwallon actually resided here or not, there is little doubt that a dwelling of some kind has stood hereabouts for centuries, although nothing remains of any previous constructions. The Cadwallon 'connection' neatly typifies the number of buildings in the region where their history reputedly encompasses events from medieval times or earlier, to great romantic effect; another example of this at Bodysgallen is its distinctive tall tower, allegedly built in the late thirteenth century as a watchtower for Conwy Castle. Its Grade I-listed-building status information states this to be unlikely, explaining that Bodysgallen is comparable in this respect to other near-contemporary houses with similar towers, such as Plas Mawr. Pevsner goes somewhat further: although the upper steps in the tower date from around 1300, their distinctive red sandstone are of the same type found at Maenan Abbey, which was bought by a descendant of the Wynns after the Dissolution. Pevsner suggests the

Bodysgallen Hall. The earliest surviving part of the house is to the left.

spiral stair might have been shipped downriver to Bodysgallen, and then re-erected as a 'romantic look-out'.

Whatever the provenance of the tower, by the mid-sixteenth century the estate was in the possession of Richard Mostyn (c. 1522–90). Richard failed to produce a son and heir, and on his death his daughter Margaret inherited Bodysgallen. Margaret married Hugh Wynn of Berthdu (d. 1614); Bodysgallen was held by the Wynns for another four generations. It is their son Robert Wynn whose initials, with those of his wife Katherine, appear on the stone dated 1620 on the south gable, the earliest part of the existing house. This comprises a large entrance hall with a drawing room above, which has seventeenth-century coats of arms of the Mostyns, Wynns and Vaughans – another important local family connected by marriage to the Wynns. The kitchen wing was added in 1730, and in 1832 the Mostyns pioneered the modern installation of a water closet.

By the end of the nineteenth century, Bodysgallen had become something of an architectural mish-mash, with its original Tudor features cluttered by Georgian sliding sash windows and Victorian brick chimneys. It was restored and enlarged around the turn of the century by Lady Augusta Mostyn for her second son, Henry; her sensitive renovations restored the vernacular architecture of the house. Henry died in 1938 and his widow in 1949, when their son Ieven inherited Bodysgallen. It fell into a long period of gradual decline until 1969, when Ieven's niece sold it for use as a private guest house. Historic House Hotels subsequently bought the property, starting their own restoration in 1980 and later opening it as a hotel. It continues to be managed by Historic House Hotels in association with the National Trust.

Corn mill of 1740 with its large iron-framed overshot waterwheel, fed from the leat running in from the left; the clover mill from 1680 is in the background.

19. Felin Isaf Mills, Pentrefelin, Glan Conwy

Watermills were introduced into Britain by the Romans. From Saxon times onwards they were an essential feature of the landscape in communities where grain was grown. The earliest component of Felin Isaf, the Clover Mill, dates from 1680; the second, larger, corn mill to 1740, and the oat kiln (oat-drying house) to 1855. They operated until 1942; this late date confirms their local significance for over 260 years. It is also an unusually complete mill complex in retaining most of its milling machinery.

Why the original mill is called the 'Clover Mill' is not known – perhaps it was once used for stripping seed off clover for use in reseeding pastures. It is built of stone,– which came from quarrying the nearby cliff. The 20-stone sacks of corn, delivered by cart and pack horses for milling, were made easier to handle by having outside steps level with the height of the carts. This first mill had a small water wheel and simple gearing driving through an axle to a four-foot millstone on the floor above. The millstone weighs three-quarters of a ton, revolving at around 100 rpm. Extant machinery within the clover mill includes a winnower for extracting chaff from the grain prior to milling, and a bolster machine used to extract bran and produce a fine flour.

Both the clover mill and the later corn mill share a leat (an open watercourse to conduct water to millwheels), the water for this deriving from a man-made millpond some 200 metres upstream. Rather than being, as it superficially appears, simply a body of water with an artificial stream emanating from it, the pond was engineered to maintain a consistent water level, including provision for redirecting flood water. The main mill retains its large iron-framed overshot waterwheel, fed from the leat and carried over the approach lane by a segmental-arched rubble bridge. The ground floor of the oat kiln has an unusual central furnace with a brick splayed and ribbed ceiling funnel – or hopper – with an access passage around four sides. Upstairs, the oats were placed for drying on cleverly-designed ceramic tiles which line the floor.

Some of the machinery in these buildings remains in working order today: for example, a millstone weighing about a ton can still be rotated by hand, and spins freely once the initial inertia is overcome. This level of precision, technical expertise and workmanship in the seventeenth and eighteenth centuries would soon be readily adapted to engineering innovations at the start of the Industrial Revolution. To be sure, steam mills would come to replace watermills and windmills, but the groundwork for the new technologies had already begun.

20. Quay House, Conwy

Quay House, or No. 10 Lower Gate Street, is better known as popular tourist destination 'The Smallest House' in Great Britain. It was built as a fisherman's cottage in the late eighteenth or early nineteenth century; building work started at either end of the quay resulting in a space in the centre against a tower of the town wall, which was soon filled in with a wall and a roof and became this tiny dwelling of two rooms. With an interior measuring only 10 feet high by 6 feet at its widest, it has neither bathroom nor kitchen. The ground floor room has a coal fire and bench under which the coal was stored. Upstairs is reached by a ladder through a trap door in the ceiling and contains a small bed.

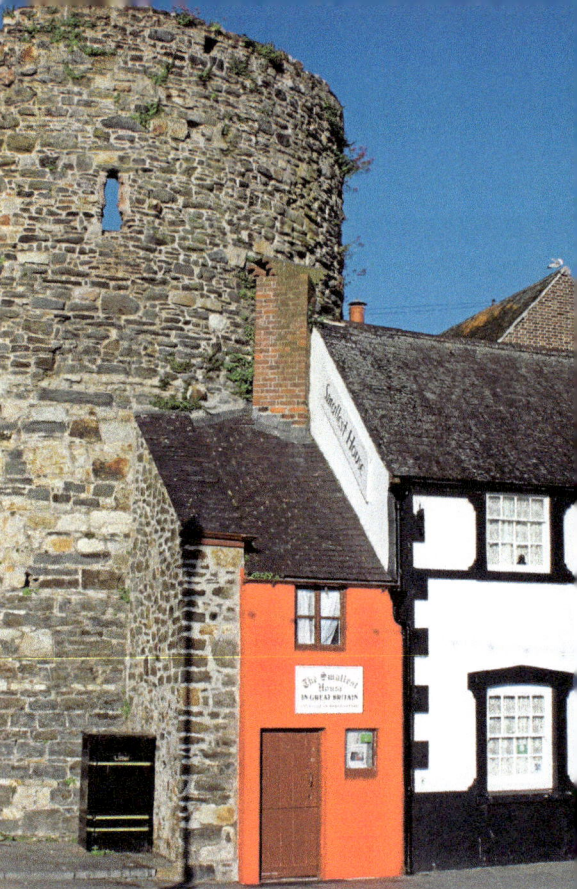

Left: The 'Smallest House' *c.* 1905, 'filling the gap' between the rows of houses on either side.

Right: The 'Smallest House'.

Quay House was occupied continually until 1900, when it was deemed by the local authority to be unsuitable for human habitation. Its last occupant was Robert Jones, a fisherman said to be 6 feet 3 inches tall and therefore unable to stand up in the rooms. It was saved from demolition that same year when Roger Dawson, first editor of the *North Wales Weekly News*, spotted its potential. He realised that if the house was the smallest in the UK it could be a huge asset to Conwy, so placed a notice in *The Times* asking if anybody knew of a smaller house anywhere in Britain. Other contenders were measured but none was found to be smaller than Quay House; it soon became a top tourist attraction, with people paying 1*d* for admission.

The Smallest House has featured in the *Guinness Book of Records* for many years, and still attracts tourists from all over the world.

21. Castle Hotel, High Street, Conwy

Today's hotel was previously two adjacent buildings: the King's Head, and a medieval guesthouse which was later developed into the Castle Hotel. The wall behind the hotel car park, dividing it from St Mary's churchyard, dates from when Aberconwy Abbey occupied

Castle Hotel, late in the nineteenth century, with a military guard of honour and many spectators lining the High Street – perhaps awaiting the arrival of the Duke and Duchess of York to Conwy in May 1899? The Harp Inn next door has long since been demolished. *Inset*: One of the many oil paintings by John Dawson Watson adorning the hotel walls. (Courtesy of the Castle Hotel)

the site. Timbers dating from around 1500 still remain behind the modern façade of the old King's Head, although the earliest surviving part of the site is found in the former stables behind the Castle, where some of the masonry may have been from the monastery.

Conwy was on the main London to Holyhead stagecoach route and both the Castle and the King's Head were coaching inns. The garden of the King's Head might have held a cockpit. These were once a key part of social life, as the sport of cockfighting was considered respectable and popular with everyone from aristocrats to rural peasants, generating furious gambling. Fighting between cockerels was banned as a sport in 1835, but it continued in practice until well into the twentieth century. Across the road, behind Plas Mawr, lie the remains of another cockpit, probably nineteenth century in origin: late in this century it was used by artist John Dawson Watson as his studio. Yorkshire-born Dawson Watson stayed in the Castle Hotel for much of his later life. A series of his Pre-Raphaelite-influenced oil paintings, based on Shakespeare's plays and characters, still adorn the Castle's interior walls – the restaurant and bar is named Dawson's in his honour. It is reputed that these paintings were executed and donated in lieu of paying for his lodgings at the hotel. Dawson Watson was also heavily involved in the hotel's 'facelift' in the 1880s, when the outside was completely rebuilt in the Jacobean style using red Ruabon brick and local flint chips.

By the 1830s, the Castle Hotel was considered to be the 5-star venue in town. It did not simply advertise for staff: an 1847 advertisement for a footman requires 'an active

Castle Hotel.

and steady man, who thoroughly understands [silver] plate cleaning, and waiting at table, also to valet a gentleman'. Such staff would doubtless have been employed at the public dinner given by the gentry of Conwy for Robert Stephenson on 17 May 1848, to celebrate the triumphant completion of his tubular railway bridge crossing the River Conwy. More than 100 tickets were sold for the dinner at a guinea (£1.05) each. The occasion was held in a temporary pavilion at the back of the hotel; the tent measured 70 feet by 24 feet, and each end was emblazoned with the gigantic initials 'RS' picked out in lamps. One speaker marvelled at the speed of the railway: 'We are now whirled along at speeds exceeding the fastest horse.'

In 1931, the Castle was bought by London-based hotel company Trust House, which eventually became Trust House Forte. In 1994 Regal Hotels took over; in 2000 the hotel was back in private hands under its present owners, the Lavin family.

22. Crossing the River Conwy: Suspension Bridge, Toll House and Railway Bridge

The River Conwy offered military security for Edward's port town; it also granted passage for seaborne traffic to voyage far down the valley. For travellers wishing to be ferried from one side to the other, though, it could be a dangerous river. In 1806 on Christmas Day, a boat conveying the *Irish Mail*, with fifteen passengers and crew aboard, was overturned in

Anchoring the bridge. From this angle the scale of Telford's task is quite apparent.

Above: Toll house.

Below: Engineering masterpieces: Telford's suspension bridge, left; Stephenson's tubular bridge, right.

heavy swell, and 'two only escaped with their lives.' Crossing it could also be frustratingly expensive. The Revd W. Bingley recorded in 1814:

> Besides the inconveniences naturally attending so wide a stream, in a place subject to […] the flowing and ebbing of tides that run sometimes very high, most of the travellers who have crossed here […] know what it is to experience the wilful delays, and the gross and barefaced impositions of the ferry-men.

He further lamented that, 'Some years ago, in contemplation to erect a bridge across the stream […] was considered to be perfectly practicable […]; but it is to be feared that this project is now entirely given up.'

Thankfully for later travellers crossing the river at Conwy, Mr Bingley was somewhat precipitate in his proclamation; in 1821 official sanction was granted for the construction of a bridge over the river. The important route from Chester to Holyhead had always been unsatisfactory: obstacles such as the Menai Straits, the headland of Penmaenmawr and the River Conwy made the journey difficult, dangerous and costly. Thomas Telford was hired to solve the engineering difficulties inherent in improving this route. As well as providing a much easier course around Penmaenmawr, he designed the Menai Straits Bridge and Conwy's Suspension Bridge – travelling from London to Ireland was no longer the struggle it had been for centuries.

Work began on the bridge in 1822 and continued for four years, at a cost of £51,000. Telford designed it to harmonise with the castle, the east barbican of which had to be demolished to provide anchorage for the wrought-iron suspension chains. The roadway, with ironwork railings either side, passes through 3-metre-wide arches in the two ashlar limestone towers from which the chains are suspended; the main span between the two towers measures 99.5 metres. The original deck probably consisted of two layers of timber planks on a light iron framework, braced with bars on its underside. In 1904, a walkway was added for pedestrian traffic.

In common with contemporary turnpike roads, a toll had to be paid for crossing the bridge – at the toll house at its eastern end. Both are now under the control of the National Trust, who have furnished the toll-keeper's lodge to show how it might have looked in 1891. The 1841 census records that John Davies was the toll collector and shared the little lodge with his wife Mary, their four young children, and a Jane Williams. His job could keep him busy twenty-four hours a day since traffic could use the bridge at any time. With the advent of the motorcar the bridge came under increasing pressure, both in terms of its carrying capacity and the congestion that was backing up into town. The last toll was taken on 30 November 1958 as the new road bridge beside it had by then been built. Since 1991 through-traffic has passed under the river within Conwy tunnel, further reducing pressure on the town.

On the other side of the suspension bridge, another novel form of transport had made its mark by 1848: the railways. As early as 1838, the Chester & Holyhead Railway was gathering support for its line linking the two towns. They appointed George Stephenson to survey the route, authorising him to build the railway in 1844. As with Telford twenty-three years previously, Stephenson was faced with problems that required major engineering works, not least in crossing the River Conwy and the Menai Straits. At Conwy the bridge's two limestone-faced towers with their crenelated turrets were designed by architect Francis Thompson to blend in with the ruins of the castle and Telford's road bridge. The line passes through a pair of parallel iron tubes, 5.5 metres above the water in single 122-metre spans, designed with help from ironmaster William Fairbairn and mathematician Professor Eaton Hodgkinson. Their final design was to be a novel use of wrought-iron tubes, pioneering the modern box girder, and Conwy Tubular Bridge was the first of its kind. The railway, passing to the south side of the castle after crossing the bridge, opened on 1 May 1848.

23. Great Orme Summit Complex, Llandudno

The Great Orme Summit Complex started life as a semaphore station in 1827, then was rebuilt and extended in 1841. Its lofty coastal position was an obvious location in the chain of such stations from Holyhead to Liverpool, picking up signals from Puffin Island off Anglesey and relaying them eastwards to the station on Mynydd Marian above Llysfaen. Apparently a message from Holyhead could be received at Liverpool in twenty-seven seconds – presumably when low cloud and sea mist allowed. By 1857 technology was changing and tenders were invited 'for constructing a line of electric telegraph between Liverpool and Holyhead.' In 1868 it was reported that 'all these stations are now disused, having given place to the electric wires which follow the course of the high roads.'

By the end of the century the Telegraph Inn, as it was now known, was experiencing problems. 1898 saw an application for a full licence objected to by Mr Roberts, a resident on the Orme, 'who said he had seen men remaining at the Telegraph Inn drunk. It was a dangerous place to get drunk.' The site, as with many pubs and inns at the time, was attracting larger concerns. In 1903 G. B. Morgan, proprietor of the Clarence Hotel, Llandudno, had 'acquired the Telegraph Inn and planned thorough alterations' to it. In 1906 it was taken over by the Great Orme Golf Club. A new Telegraph Hotel was built in

Telegraph Hotel, 1908. *Inset*: Semaphore Station after the rebuild of 1841.

Great Orme Summit Complex.

1908 by the golf links' proprietor Mr McDonald, and a new clubhouse formed part of this building. It was not to everyone's liking: one observer complained about 'the spoliation of the grand old headland by the modern builder and engineer and speculator.' The golf course played on until the onset of the Second World War, when the hotel was requisitioned by the RAF and used as a radar station.

With the end of hostilities the building, now the Great Orme International Sporting and Holiday Centre, was put on the market in 1949. The old golf course reverted to pasture land and the hotel sold in 1952 to world middleweight boxing champion Randolph Turpin. He renamed it the Summit Hotel and opened the popular Randy's Bar; he also gave boxing shows in an outdoor ring. Unfortunately, by 1961 he had been served with an Income Tax writ for £16,000 and not long afterwards Llandudno Urban Council bought him out. The café was then let to Forte's.

Nowadays, the Summit Complex offers visitors a café/restaurant, a boxing-themed bar based on Randolph Turpin and a gift shop. Nearby, the Country Park Visitor Centre exhibits information on the nature reserve, which encompasses much of the summit of the Great Orme.

24. New York Cottages, Bangor Road, Penmaenmawr

By the 1830s the Industrial Revolution was well underway and certain urban centres – for example, Merthyr Tydfil in south Wales – were growing staggeringly quickly, attracting thousands of migrants from rural areas to what were often insanitary housing conditions. However, with no local coal or iron deposits and no surrounding industrial heartland, this revolution largely bypassed Conwy. During this period the population in the area covered by Conwy's Poor Law Union had increased from 6,586 in 1801 to just 9,703 by 1831; Merthyr's had risen from 8,803 to 23,618.

The parish of Dwygyfylchi mirrored this slow growth, having a population of 281 in 1801, rising to 444 by 1831. It continued a pastoral way of life, largely untouched for centuries. However, by 1831 this was about to change. Although no coal or iron lay underground, the igneous rock that had triggered a Neolithic hand axe 'factory' was to

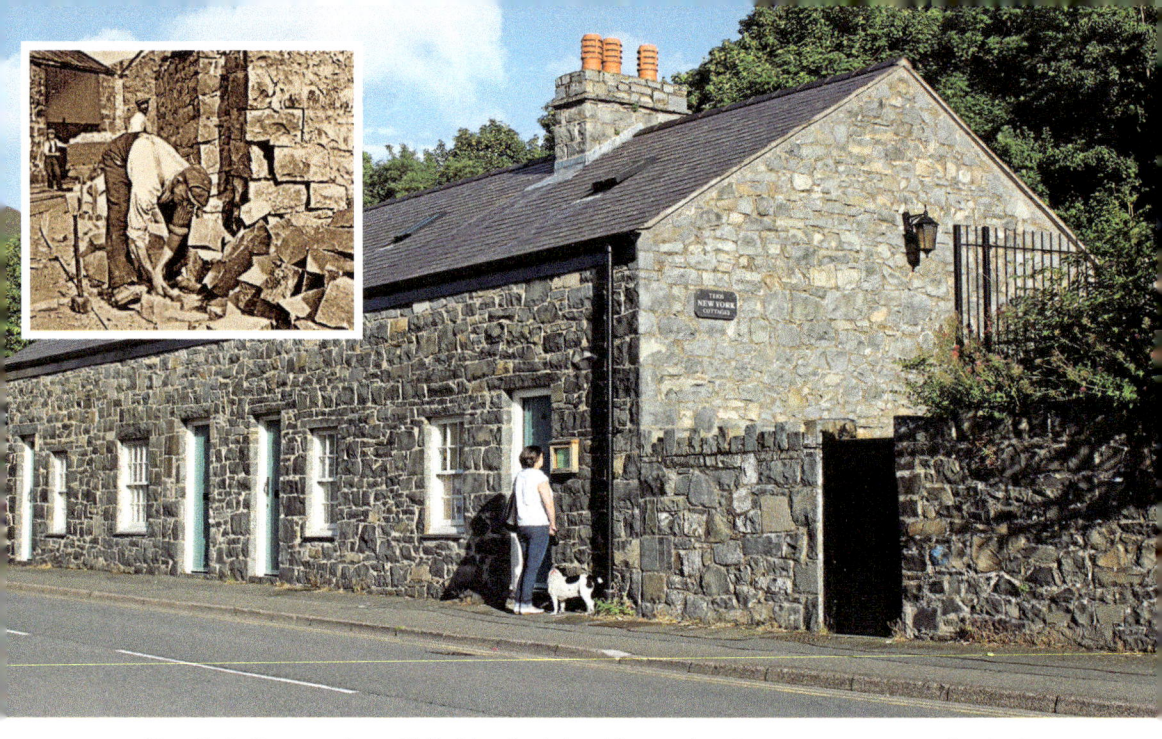

New York Cottages. *Inset*: Skilled but back-breaking work: a Penmaenmawr sett-maker in the nineteenth century. (Courtesy of Penmaenmawr Museum)

bring it into the world of industrial development and associated population growth. By the end of the century the population had grown to 3,500, with the prime employers being the quarries on the mountain summits above the new villages of Penmaenan and Penmaenmawr.

Quarrying for the stone, primarily for use as setts (road paving slabs), began with leases granted in 1833. As this progressed towards being a fully industrial venture extra workers were required. Initially many were housed in barrack-style accommodation at nearby Plas Celyn, a former gentleman's retreat – in 1841 seventy-four people resided there, 10 per cent of the parish's population. New York Cottages (originally six, of which four remain) were built by the owners of Graiglwyd Quarry for quarrymen and their families in 1849–50, just as a slump in orders damaged profitability. Redundancies followed and tradition has it that one of the workmen, when asked what the name of the cottages should be, answered New York 'as everyone was thinking of going there rather than coming to live here'.

In 1851 the cottages were occupied by a mariner from Anglesey, with his wife and seven children; a Scottish blacksmith with his wife and seven children; a further blacksmith, from Llandygai near Bangor, with his wife and son; a Denbigh-born widow and pauper (on parish out relief) with a son and a lodger; an Irish agricultural labourer, with his wife and eight children; and lastly the only 'local', an agricultural labourer with his wife and four children. The range of birthplaces of these heads of households is suggestive of a new community, attracting incomers from far and wide, as was the case in the larger industrial developments elsewhere – notwithstanding the apparently greater attraction of New York. Given the extremely limited space within each cottage we can only guess at the living arrangements for the larger families.

The railway arrived in 1848, and once the depression of the 1850s was over Penmaenmawr's quarries expanded apace, resulting in much new housing. With the railways came another source of income as visitors and tourists arrived, with a subsequent building of guesthouses and a further modification of the area's identity. During this period Penmaenmawr's most distinguished regular guest was William Ewart Gladstone, who served four terms as Liberal prime minister.

By 1865 other ventures associated with industrialism were beginning. A room in No. 2 New York Cottages was converted into a store for the newly created 'Penmaenmawr Co-operative and Industrial Society', where it remained until moving to larger premises in 1887. Today, No. 4 is home to Penmaenmawr Museum, where the history of the parish from its earliest days is displayed to enlighten visitors.

25. Conwy Visitor Centre (former National School), Rose Hill Street

Just as with the rest of England and Wales, education in the Conwy area was something of a hit-and-miss affair until the Elementary Education Act of 1880 made it compulsory for all children aged between five and ten to attend school. This was further reinforced in 1891, when the Free Education Act made grants available to all schools to enable them to stop charging for basic education; two years later, the school leaving age was raised to eleven. Before this time, education for children was generally limited to those whose parents could afford to pay for it, and there were many different types of school offering a wide variety of non-standardised education. Conwy had its fair share of these, including charity schools (one of which was based in Plas Mawr), a workhouse school, 'dame' schools and diverse privately-run institutions.

Conwy Visitor Centre.

National schools were created by the National Society for Promoting Religious Education. Formed in 1811, it stipulated that the national religion should be the main thing taught to poor children and aimed to found a church school in every parish; by 1851 there were 12,000 across England and Wales. On 18 December 1837, Conwy town council decided that 'Scubor fawr (i.e. *ysgubor fawr*, Welsh for 'great barn') and the land upon which it is situated be given for building a National School and house for the master.' The land – on the south-east side of Rose Hill Street – was paid for by Sir David Erskine of Pwllycrochan, and the cost of the building (£380) came from voluntary contributions. Construction began in 1838; it opened as a national school for boys and girls in 1840. In 1887 the boys moved to a new school building (now used as St Mary's church hall) on the opposite side of the street, which was funded by Albert Wood of Bodlondeb, a major benefactor and patron of education in Conwy. In the same year, the infants housed in Plas Mawr joined the girls in the national school at Rose Hill Street.

In 1927 the girls and the infants moved to the new Bodlondeb School, purpose-built on land on the Bodlondeb Estate also given by Albert Wood. The old Girls' National School building in Rose Hill Street appears to have remained empty until 1978, when it was opened as the Conwy Visitor Centre, which continues to trade today.

26. Grand Hotel, Happy Valley Road, Llandudno

The growth in the popularity of sea bathing grew from the perceived health benefits of medicinal springs. By the mid-eighteenth century, various books had been published extolling the virtues of both immersing oneself in and drinking sea water, and this practice became fashionable as a treatment for many diseases. By Victorian times, the spread of the railways along with the burgeoning craze for sea bathing had created a new phenomenon: the British seaside resort. Llandudno was developed with just this aim in mind – a respectable holiday destination for the upper-middle classes – and the requisite bathhouse was constructed against the eastern side of the Great Orme in 1855. The previous year, St George's Hotel had been the first modern building on Llandudno's promenade; various other hotels followed, including, in 1860, the 'Hydropathic Establishment' (now the Hydro Hotel) which offered such fashionable water cures as 'four Russian vapour and two commodious and well-appointed Turkish baths, the seaweed or ozone bath'. Perhaps, as an alternative to these delights – or indeed, as competition to them – the bathhouse complex was comprehensively extended in the late 1870s to form the Baths Hotel. This was substantially reconstructed in 1901, and reopened as the Grand Hotel the following year.

With its 158 bedrooms, large ballroom and opulent reception rooms, the Grand was aptly named. The largest hotel in Wales, it dominated the western end of Llandudno Bay and continued to attract well-heeled guests until the Second World War, when it became the base for two Inland Revenue departments. Its pre- and post-war clientele included a number of prominent politicians, who stayed there when their party conferences were held in Llandudno: Lloyd George, Sir Oswald Mosley, Anthony Eden, Harold Wilson and Edward Heath all appear in the hotel's registers, along with Winston Churchill, who paid his last visit to the town in 1948.

Above: Bathhouse and Pier Pavilion, *c.* 1890. *Inset*: Bathhouse 1855, predating the pier and sea wall.

Below: Grand Hotel.

The hotel was run by Butlins during the 1980s and 1990s and was acquired by Britannia Hotels in 2004. Today, the Grand has 162 bedrooms, a ballroom, two restaurants and a bar, and remains the largest hotel in north Wales.

27. Camera Obscura, Great Orme, Llandudno

A camera obscura (Latin for 'dark room') is an optical device from which photography developed. An Arab physicist, Ibn al-Haytham, published his *Book of Optics* in 1021 AD, and created the first pinhole camera after observing how light travelled through a window shutter. He is also believed to have invented the first camera obscura: a box or room with a pinhole in one side. Light from an external scene passes through the hole and strikes an inside surface where it is reproduced, inverted but with the original colours and perspective. The image can be projected onto paper and then drawn over to produce a highly accurate representation. Mirrors can be used to project a right-side-up image, and a lens is now often used instead of a pinhole.

Llandudno's Camera Obscura, on the eponymous 'Camera Hill', is one of the town's lesser-known attractions and the third such octagonal building on the same site. The first

Camera Obscura.

small wooden construction was built around 1860 by Lot Williams, one of Llandudno's first postmen. It quickly became an attraction for holidaying Victorians, who would marvel at the panoramic views of the town created by this scientific wonder, Lot's 'Magic Shed'. The second Camera Obscura was built in 1994 by local taxi-driver Jack Shields to replace the original, which was destroyed by fire in 1966. It was replaced by the council in 2001 by the current building to celebrate the millennium but stood empty for a number of years after Mr Shields died in 2007, reopening in 2013 after restoration by his nephew. One of only seven left in the UK, the Camera Obscura still uses a system of mirrors and lens to project an extensive 360° panorama onto a circular table for visitors to view.

28. Guildhall, Rose Hill Street, Conwy

It is claimed that buildings have stood on the site of the Guildhall since the thirteenth century, although no records remain of their previous function. The Guildhall was built in two phases: the first, in 1863, incorporated a tall gabled range facing Rose Hill Street, with a porch and turret facing Castle Square. The entrance was reached up stone steps from Castle Square. The Council Chamber was built in the style of a Gothic

Administrative centres old and new: castle to the left, Guildhall to the right. (© Crown copyright (2016) Welsh Government)

Gothic-influenced entrance to the Guildhall.

hall, with an appropriately grand fireplace. The Guildhall was used as the town hall by Conwy Corporation until 1899, when the newly built Civic Hall on Castle Street was officially opened.

The building was extended in 1925, when the entrance steps were removed and a new porch with elaborate stone carving was added. A new council chamber was added to its left-hand side; internally it has a hammerbeam roof with coloured plaster panels. The former council chamber then became a mayor's parlour. The Guildhall is now home to Conwy Town Council and houses an impressive collection of oil paintings, including local landscapes by members of the nearby Royal Cambrian Academy. Three mayoral portraits, dating from the late nineteenth century, hang in the council chamber, the most notable of which is of William Hughes, the first mayor of Conwy, painted by John Dawson Watson – an artist who spent his later years in the town.

29. Plas Pwllycrochan, Pwllycrochan Avenue, Colwyn Bay

Driving to Colwyn Bay from the direction of Llandudno, the large white castellated building perched on the wooded hill above the town is a noticeable landmark. Originally known as Plas Pwllycrochan, it played a significant role in the development of Colwyn Bay as a fashionable resort in the second half of the nineteenth century.

Scottish baronet and major landowner Sir David Erskine inherited the Pwllycrochan estate – much of what is now Colwyn Bay – through his marriage in 1821 to Jane Silence Williams. Together, they demolished much of the original late seventeenth-century house and built their own home on the site. After Sir John's death in 1841, Lady Erskine kept the estate going, but in 1865 their eldest son Thomas sold it off in lots at auction. The bulk was bought by businessman John Pender, who intended to develop a seaside resort for the affluent classes of the Midlands and North West. The mansion was leased to Pender's agent John Porter, who converted it into the Pwllycrochan Hotel in 1866. However, insolvency forced Pender to sell up, and in 1875 a consortium of Manchester businessmen bought much of the estate and formed the 'Colwyn Bay and Pwllycrochan Estate Company', which continued with the planning and development of the new resort town. John Porter bought the freehold of the Pwllycrochan Hotel in the same year. He was very much involved with Colwyn Bay's public life, and was referred to in his obituary in the local press in 1899 as 'the Father of Colwyn Bay'.

A 1911 advertisement for the hotel states it as having 'ground floor suites, electric light, billiards, bathing, tennis and golf', and in 1937 it held a Grand Coronation Ball in celebration of the coronation of George VI, tickets for which cost 15s 6d (77½p) and included supper. During the Second World War the hotel was one of many buildings in the town to be taken over by the Ministry of Food, which in 1940 evacuated its entire staff of around 5,000 from Whitehall to Colwyn Bay. The Pwllycrochan Hotel reopened in 1948 after extensive renovations. It was clearly a select establishment: a 1949 advert for its weekly dinner dances, costing 12s 6d (62½p) per person, stated 'Evening Dress is Preferred'. Unfortunately, changing trends in British holidays meant that business faltered, and in 1952 the hotel closed for good. The mansion and grounds were bought by Rydal School in 1953 to house its junior department; following a merger of Rydal with Penrhos College in 1995, it is now known as Rydal Penrhos Preparatory School.

Plas Pwllycrochan.

3c. Harbour Master's Office, Conwy

The Grade II-listed harbour master's office on Conwy quay is built against the Postern Tower of the medieval town wall. Its listing description states it was built in the second half of the nineteenth century; however, trade directories from the 1870s refer to it as an 'antique building', suggesting it is perhaps older than supposed.

Whatever its provenance, the building was used throughout the nineteenth century as Conwy's Customs House. Conwy had been a busy port for many centuries: exports included slate, salt, potatoes and potash – the ash of seaweed used in soap production – while all imported goods such as coal, timber and groceries had to have their correct duties paid. However, the spread of the railways meant that maritime trade in Conwy decreased. Caernarfon became the 'Customs Port' for the whole north Wales coastline, and Conwy was downgraded to 'creek' status – although it had a brief resurgence, when it was reported in the local press in 1897 that the Board of Customs had raised Conwy to 'second-class port', which 'speaks well for the improving condition of local trade'.

Nonetheless, activity on Conwy quay became increasingly dominated by fishing, removing the need for a Customs presence. By the early twentieth century, the Customs House building was being used by the Ministry of Labour as the local Employment Exchange. The ground floor was used at various times as a meeting place for the First

Harbourmaster's Office.

Conwy Scouts, and after the Second World War it became permanent home to Conwy's harbour master and his staff. Their work today is concentrated mainly on the leisure craft and activities in the estuary, harbour and two local marinas.

31. Capel Carmel, Chapel Street, Conwy

Nonconformity was a significant influence in Wales from the eighteenth to the twentieth centuries, and Nonconformist places of worship are so much a part of the Welsh landscape that they are almost the national architecture of Wales. The early meeting places were domestic – private homes or barns – where the often makeshift pulpit would hold centre stage to emphasise the main purpose of the worship: the preaching. The 'golden age' of the Welsh Nonconformist chapel was the nineteenth century: during the first half, new chapels were reportedly built at the rate of one every eight days. Chapels were at the heart of community life for many thousands of people, and they remain an important part of Welsh cultural heritage.

Calvinistic Methodism was born out of the eighteenth-century Methodist Revival in Wales and survives today as the Presbyterian Church of Wales. It is the only one of the

Capel Carmel.

Nonconformist denominations to be indigenous to Wales, with no English equivalent. The original Carmel Calvinistic Methodist Chapel in Conwy was built in 1785. It was rebuilt in 1826, and again in 1875 by Richard Owens, the second most prolific chapel architect in Wales (after Thomas Thomas), and the favoured late-nineteenth-century architect of the Calvinistic Methodists. In all he designed around 300 chapels, largely in north Wales. By the time Owens rebuilt the Carmel Chapel, the design of Nonconformist places of worship had moved away from the domestic and increasingly favoured more 'architectural' gabled fronts, with Gothic or classical façades being particularly fashionable. With its symmetrical gabled end frontage, pilasters and balustrading, Carmel Chapel is resolutely in the classical style.

32. Llandudno Pier

Britain's first seaside pier opened at Ryde on the Isle of Wight in 1814. Dozens of others followed, and before long no self-respecting fashionable seaside resort was complete without its own 'pleasure' pier, where holidaymakers could stroll and take

Above: Llandudno pier, *c.* 1890.

Below: Crowning the May Queen in the Pier Pavilion, before 1914.

Llandudno pier.

the reputedly healthy sea air. Llandudno's first pier was constructed by the St George's Harbour & Railway, which in 1858 had just completed its branch line from Llandudno Junction to Llandudno. The original pier was opened this year as part of an ambitious scheme to create a major port in Llandudno Bay. In 1859 it was severely damaged by a major storm, which was estimated to be the worst to hit the Irish Sea during the nineteenth century. It became known as the 'Royal Charter Storm', due to the steam clipper of that name, which foundered off the east coast of Anglesey in the early hours of 26 October with a loss of over 450 lives. In all, the storm claimed 233 vessels and more than 800 souls.

Although Llandudno pier was repaired following the great storm it was only to survive a further sixteen years. It proved to be just too short to serve the increasing number of steamers that could only access it at high tide, and business was being lost to the burgeoning port of Holyhead. The decision was taken to replace the pier with a more suitable iron structure designed for the tourist trade, in a period when Llandudno was developing as a stylish holiday destination. It took just over one year to construct; at 1,234 feet in length it was considerably longer than the original structure, and it was opened to the general public on 1 August 1877. An extension was later built that passed the Baths Hotel (now the Grand) to the promenade. This took the pier's overall length to an impressive 2,295 feet, making it Wales' longest pier – an honour it still holds today.

In 1881 the pier's owners made the decision to replace the sundeck pavilion at its shore end with a purpose-built theatre, to take advantage of Llandudno's increasing popularity as a seaside resort. The ornate, three-storey Pier Pavilion Theatre was just over 200 feet in length and could seat 2,000. Unusually, it had a swimming pool in its basement – in its time it was the largest indoor swimming pool of its kind, and refilled itself twice daily with the changing tides. Unfortunately, this brought serious problems with the quality of the water, and the pool was filled in shortly after opening. The Pavilion was due to be opened in the spring of 1883, but a violent storm in the January caused severe damage to the glass roof. It was eventually decided to replace this with a more traditional, robust lead roof, involving a major reworking of the structure. The new Pier Pavilion Theatre finally opened its doors in September 1886; the small orchestra led by French musician Jules Rivière, which had previously played to visitors on the pier head, made its home in the Pier Pavilion and before long had more than doubled in size. The Pavilion orchestra continued to entertain summer guests at promenade concerts until its final disbandment in 1974. Variety shows began in 1936, and became a draw for many 'household names'. Sadly, the growing popularity of television meant that live variety shows began to lose their appeal, and attendance gradually declined until the theatre was closed in 1984. Various schemes to revive the Pier Pavilion came to naught, and the building grew increasingly neglected and dilapidated until it became the victim of an arson attack in 1994; now all that remains of the Pier Pavilion is a hole in the ground and a few remnants of the wrought-iron veranda and other embellishments.

At a time when many piers have been lost with the rise of cheaper foreign flights and the resultant decline in some seaside resorts, the Grade II-listed Llandudno Pier continues to draw many visitors all year round.

33. Toll Houses, Marine Drive, Llandudno

The original route around the Great Orme was a pedestrian path, named Cust's Path after Reginald Cust, a trustee of the Mostyn Estate. It was engineered in the cliff faces in the 1850s, and was so exposed and vertiginous that Gladstone complained that he had to be blindfolded in order to be led along it. In 1872, the Great Orme's Head Marine Drive Co. was inaugurated to convert the path to a carriage drive for horse-drawn vehicles. Work on the drive, perched halfway down the limestone cliffs and constructed with difficulty, began in September 1875 under the supervision of engineers Hedworth Lee and George Felton. It was completed at a cost of £14,000 in 1878, when the two toll house lodges were also built.

Happy Valley Lodge retains its original toll office, where today's visitors still part with cash to drive the four or so miles around the Great Orme and enjoy the spectacular views. West Lodge, at the far end of the drive, has had its toll office demolished. Designed by the Mostyns' architect of the time, Abraham Foulkes, both are built of local stone and resemble miniature castles, complete with towers and battlements; they are both private dwellings now called, rather confusingly, The Toll House and Tollgate House respectively.

Above: Probably not the best day to be conveyed around Marine Drive in a horse-drawn carriage Happy Valley Toll House, *c.* 1900. *Inset*: Cust's Path in the early 1850s.

Below: Happy Valley Lodge and Toll House. *Inset*: West Lodge with Toll House in the 1930s.

34. Bodlondeb, Bangor Road, Conwy

The estate at Bodlondeb (Welsh for 'contentment') originally belonged to the Hollands, a local family who owned much of Conwy during the eighteenth century. Surrounded by woods and parkland, the original house was a family home, built in 1742. The current house dates from 1877 and was built for Arthur Wood, whose family had amassed its wealth from manufacturing anchors and shipping chains in Saltney, near Chester. The company's anchors were selected for use on the *SS Great Eastern*, Brunel's massive 22,500-ton steamship from the late 1850s that was so far ahead of her time that her length (nearly 700 feet) and tonnage would remain unmatched for four more decades. Wood's Patent Anchor was displayed in the Great Exhibition (1851) and was used on Royal Navy ships and other vessels.

Notable visitors to the house included former British Prime Minister David Lloyd George and composer Sir Edward Elgar; it is rumoured that Queen Victoria expressed a desire to visit Bodlondeb, but that the house was too small to accommodate the royal entourage. Albert Wood achieved prominence in the area, being at various times a Justice of the Peace, the Mayor of Conwy and the first Freeman of the Borough. He also presented to the town the statue of Llewelyn the Great and fountain in Lancaster Square to mark the installation of a new water supply system.

Bodlondeb and its 60 acres stayed in the possession of the Wood family until Albert's death in 1936, when it was compulsorily purchased by the council in order to provide public parkland and civic offices. It was officially reopened for this purpose in July 1937 by Lloyd George and is now the headquarters of Conwy County Borough Council.

Bodlondeb.

35. St Paul's Church, Mostyn Avenue, Craig-y-Don, Llandudno

The life of Prince Albert Victor, Duke of Clarence and Avondale, although short, has attracted more than its fair share of posthumous controversy. Born in 1864 and named after his grandparents, Queen Victoria and Prince Albert, he was the eldest son of the then Prince of Wales, who acceded to the British throne in 1901 as Edward VII. Albert Victor, the heir apparent, would have gone on to become king himself had he not died at the tender age of twenty-eight, a victim of a worldwide influenza pandemic that swept across Britain in the winter of 1891–92. Only a few weeks before his death he had become engaged to Princess Mary of Teck, a union reportedly engineered by his grandmother, Queen Victoria. The following year, Mary married Albert Victor's younger brother George – now first in line to the throne – and became Queen Mary when her husband was crowned George V in 1910.

Albert Victor's untimely death stunned the nation, and the obituaries and eulogies that followed were full of respect and praise. However, later royal biographers began to cast doubt on elements of his character and mental faculties, and therefore his suitability as prospective king. It was not long before the conspiracy theorists took these ideas and ran with them. Among the more colourful suggestions was that the prince was 'disposed of': that he died of poisoning rather than flu, or that he didn't die at all and was confined to a lunatic asylum, or taken overseas and hidden. He has even been suggested, in a book published some seventy years after his death, as a possible Jack the Ripper, the infamous London mass-murderer whose true identity has never been established; however, contemporary court records show that Albert Victor was many miles away from London at the times of each of the murders, and other rumours about his life (and death) have similarly been shown to be based on somewhat lurid speculation rather than facts.

Less than four weeks after his death, a meeting at the Imperial Hotel in Llandudno resolved that a proposed new church in Craig-y-Don should be built as a memorial to the late prince. The town of Llandudno, unusually, is split into two parishes: Llandudno itself, to the west and in the diocese of Bangor; and Llanrhos parish – in the St Asaph diocese – to the east, with its mother church, St Hilary's, nearly 2 miles from the centre of Llandudno. By 1891, Llandudno had become an extremely popular tourist destination, with some 4,000 summer visitors expected that year. With Llanrhos parish church only accommodating 140 worshippers and nowhere for services in east Llandudno, it was clear that a new place of worship was needed; in June 1891 the bishop of St Asaph commended the building of a new church in Craig-y-Don, adding that it would be 'largely for English visitors to Llandudno'. Lord Mostyn, who donated the site, wrote to the Prince and Princess of Wales proposing that the new church be named after their late son, and a response from their private secretary stated that the royal couple gave their 'cordial adhesion to the suggestion'.

The plans for the new church were drawn up by John Oldrid Scott, son of the eminent architect Sir Gilbert Scott. It was built in sections: the cornerstones were laid in 1893 by Lady Augusta Mostyn, with the memorial stone of the nave laid in April 1895 by the Duchess of Teck, who was accompanied by her daughter Mary, former fiancée of the late Duke of Clarence. The nave was opened for public worship later that year. Two side aisles were added in 1899, and the chancel in 1901. The church of St Paul's Craig-y-Don – the

Duke of Clarence Memorial Church – was consecrated by the bishop of St Asaph on 4 September that year.

The original plans included a large tower and spire, which together would stand over 270 feet; however, this was never built because the structure would have been too heavy for the building's foundations. A handsome church in the Gothic Revival style, St Paul's is, by any standards, a fitting royal memorial: its lofty nave is almost 100 feet long and 64 feet high, and contains eight columns of fine black Northumberland fossil marble, a pink alabaster pulpit and green marble font, and an ornately carved oak altar and reredos. The three-manual William Hill organ was dedicated in 1910 and cost £1,000, which was donated entirely by a Mrs Walch in memory of her late husband. Today, music at St Paul's is still important. It has one of the few traditional Anglican four-part robed choirs left in north Wales, and holds fundraising concerts throughout the year.

Duke and Duchess of Teck arriving at St Paul's Church with their daughter Princess Mary, April 1895. (© St Paul's Church, Craig-y-Don, Llandudno)

Above: St Paul's Church. *Inset*: Prince Albert Victor, Duke of Clarence and Avondale, 1889, photograph by Lafayette. (© National Portrait Gallery, London)

Below: Musical events are a popular feature of St Paul's during the summer.

36. Former Bodlondeb Castle Hotel, Church Walks, Llandudno

Among the sturdy, irreproachably Victorian hotels, guesthouses and villas of Church Walks is what appears to be a Gothic fantasy of a Scottish baronial pile – Bodlondeb Castle. Commissioned as a private residence in the 1890s by a wealthy visitor, no expense was spared in its construction. Italian craftsmen joined the local builder Thomas Pugh Davies to create a marble baronial hall-style atrium with translucent marble pillars, a Gothic-style staircase, and fine stained-glass windows bearing the coats of arms of the legendary fifteen

Former Bodlondeb Castle Hotel.

tribes of north Wales. When the client viewed his finished residence he was reportedly disappointed with the lack of land surrounding the property, and declared himself no longer interested. Local rumour has it that the client was the Prince of Wales (later Edward VII), although there is no evidence for this.

Bodlondeb Castle remained in the Davies family until 1931 when it was sold to Methodist Holiday Homes Ltd, who opened it as a temperance hotel. The former Caersalem Chapel behind Bodlondeb was purchased in 1934 as an annexe to the hotel. It had ceased function as a place of worship in 1875 when it became a school; a plaque in the gable of its doorway states that William Morris 'Billy' Hughes, the seventh prime minister of Australia (1915–23), was educated there.

The hotel remained open to guests during the Second World War, despite having around forty civil servants from the evacuated Inland Revenue billeted there. Sadly, the changing fashions in holiday destinations took their toll on the hotel's trade, and Bodlondeb Castle Hotel closed in 2005 when the occupancy rate had fallen to an unviable 32 per cent. It was bought by a property development company from the north-west of England and sympathetically converted into eight luxury apartments. The entire building, including the former chapel, is Grade II listed.

37. Victoria Tram Station, Church Walks, Llandudno

The starting point for the Great Orme Tramway was built in 1904 and named after the former Victoria Hotel, which was demolished to make way for the tramway. The tramway itself, an engineering marvel of its day, is the only funicular (cable-hauled) tramway still operating on British public roads. Its history began in 1898, when the Great Orme Tramways Act was passed. The lower section was opened in July 1902, when the first paying passengers were seen off by the town band playing 'God Save the King'. Its original purpose was to transport passengers, goods and parcels up and down the Great Orme, and even had to carry coffins to the Halfway Station for burial at St Tudno's churchyard. No concession was made for grief:

Victoria Station.

mourners were charged full fare, plus 2s 6d (12 ½p) for transporting the coffin. The upper section opened the following year, taking visitors almost to the summit of the Great Orme to admire the views.

The line was designed to work as two halves, to match the capacity of the power equipment available at the time to haul the tramcars up the steep gradient. The lower section is just under 800 metres in length, the upper 756 metres. Each section has two tramcars, which pass each other at the midpoint. The steepest part is the first section out of Victoria Station, where the gradient is up to 1 in 3.6. The only major incident on the tramway occurred in 1932, when a component broke on a tramcar descending the steepest section; the car derailed and crashed into a stone wall, killing the driver and a young girl and injuring several passengers. Automatic brakes were introduced in 1934, and it was converted from steam power to electric drive in 1957.

Between 1999 and 2000 the tramway received £2 million from the EU and the Heritage Lottery Fund for refurbishment, while Conwy Borough Council committed a further £2 million for its preservation. Today, Victoria Station is the starting point for around 160,000 passengers per year on the tramway.

38. Oriel Mostyn Gallery, Vaughan Street, Llandudno

In the late nineteenth and early twentieth century a number of imposing public buildings were added to the townscape of Llandudno. Many were designed by architect and surveyor Dr George Alfred Humphreys, chief agent of the Mostyn Estate from 1889 until his death in 1948. His creations include the Grand Theatre (1901), Seilo Calvinistic Methodist Chapel with its splendid towers (1905), the library (1908–10), and the concrete colonnade leading to Happy Valley (1932). Humphreys also designed a number of buildings on the east side of Vaughan Street, three of which have similar orange terracotta façades in a 'northern Renaissance' style: Imperial Buildings (1898), the Post Office (1904), and standing between them, Mostyn Art Gallery (1901).

Since the eighteenth century and the rise of industrialism, charitable and philanthropic activity had become a widespread cultural practice, usually directed at the improvement of the lower classes. Mostyn Art Gallery was built under the patronage of Lady Augusta Mostyn (1830–1912), with the aid of a number of wealthy Llandudno citizens, to be a cultural centre for Llandudno's residents and to encourage the development of art and craft. For the first three years following its opening, the Gwynedd Ladies' Art Society (of which Lady Augusta was president and patron) exhibited its work in the gallery, though in 1903 the members were asked to make way for new developments.

Lady Augusta also envisioned the setting up of a 'School of Art, Science and Technical Classes'; this was duly installed by 1903. In 1904, both day and evening classes and guest lectures were being provided, funded by fees, grants, subscriptions and donations, with student numbers rising to 159 by September. While the school was relatively successful, matters 'behind the scenes' were not progressing so well. It was felt by some that the classes could be too elementary and that the available equipment should be of a higher standard. From 1904 attempts were made to have the school taken over by the County Education Authority, or to have its £100-per-year grant increased; neither were successful. Three years later the teaching of many subjects moved to Lloyd Street School, with the gallery retaining

Above: The orange terracotta façade of Oriel Mostyn Gallery.

Below: In the summer of 2016 works were exhibited on disciplines taught in the original school: 'metalwork', 'light and shade' and, shown here, 'brush drawing' (Camille Henrot).

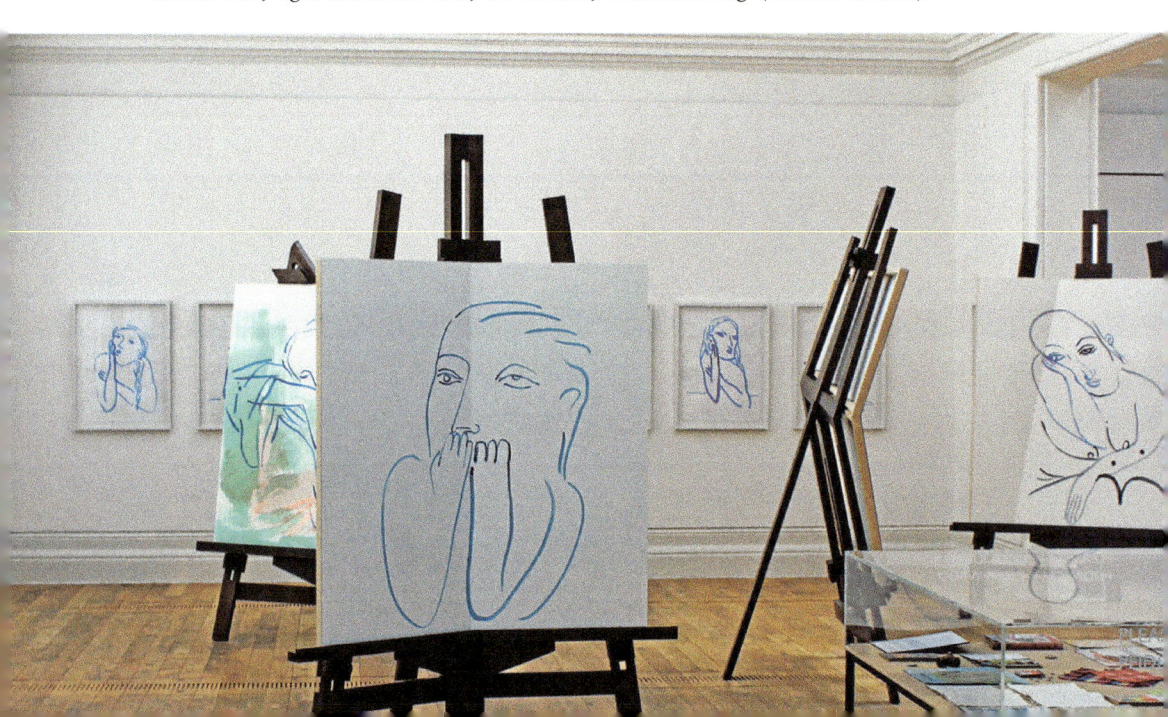

art classes covering topics and techniques such as oil painting, brush drawing, light and shade, woodcarving, metalwork and clay modelling. While some students could be viewed as 'working class', many were teachers or of similar occupations, or were not working at all – one student was described as 'a bank manager's daughter', perhaps not the clientele originally anticipated at the school's inception.

The art exhibitions held at the gallery were, however, successful. One in 1906, opened by Lady Augusta, displayed 'ancient and modern pictures, pastels, cartoons for stained glass by Sir Edward Burne Jones and Ford Madox Brown'. Also on show were examples of Delia Robbia Pottery from Birkenhead, lent to the exhibition by the pottery's founder and Llandudno resident Mr Harold Rathbone, a painter born of the Arts and Crafts Movement inspired by William Morris. Rathbone had trained a group of local young people in his native Liverpool in the art of pottery, a philanthropic endeavour which chimed with the aims of Mostyn Gallery.

Notwithstanding the success of its many exhibitions, the gallery closed around 1912. The building took on quite different functions for the next six decades, first being requisitioned as a drill hall. After the First World War, it had various commercial and storage uses before being requisitioned again in 1939, this time as a storage facility for the Inland Revenue who were evacuated to Llandudno. The American Medical Corps set up a café there, 'The Donut Dug Out', frequented by many of the large contingent of American servicemen stationed in the town. After the war, the building became Wagstaff's Piano and Music Gallery. By 1976 proposals were being made to return the place to its original function – as an art gallery serving north Wales. It reopened as such, renamed Oriel Mostyn Gallery, in 1979.

Once reopened, the gallery quickly gained national and international recognition for the high standards maintained in exhibiting a wide range of the best of contemporary art, by artists both local and from across the world. New exhibitions are arranged every two months, which can be accessed freely by the local community and visitors to the area. In 2010 the buildings were brought together in a design by architect Dominic Williams, giving five galleries in which a variety of art forms can be displayed: a shop and a café complete the ensemble.

39. Town Hall, Lloyd Street, Llandudno

Following Lord Mostyn's acquisition of the Morfa in 1849, through an Enclosure Act and the subsequent growth of Llandudno as a resort, much of the planning for the town rested with twenty-one Llandudno Improvement Commissioners whose office was on Church Walks. As early as 1853 the commissioners were aware that the town needed a town hall; it may be assumed that they were conscious of the imposing and grandiose town halls being erected in the growing industrial towns of the north-west of England. Yet Llandudno was not to have its own until 1902. The debates and proposals for Llandudno's town hall can be followed through a selection of reports of the commissioners' meetings in *The north Wales Chronicle and Advertiser*:

1853: 'it is proposed to authorise the said Commissioners [...] to construct, regulate, and maintain, a Town Hall, with assembly, news, and other rooms, for the use of the inhabitants.'

Above: Llandudno Town Hall, 1902.

Below: Llandudno Town Hall.

1859: 'plots of most desirable Building Land, centrally situate near the Market Hall, and the sites of the intended Town Hall and Church.'
1868: 'Mr Thos. Parry moved that the question of purchasing or leasing land for the erection of a Town Hall [...] be referred to the Inspection Committee.'
1879: 'A letter was read from Mr St John Charlton, offering, on behalf of the Mostyn estate, to give site for a town hall, and granting a lease of the large yard for 999 years at an annual rental of £75.'
1888: 'Tenders for the erection of a new Market were to hand, but [...] the matter was deferred, pending the further consideration of the proposed Town Hall, Public Offices, &c., scheme.'
1894: 'The Proposed Municipal Buildings: the piece of land given by Lord Mostyn in Lloyd Street had been valued at £2,000, and the question had already been left in abeyance for years.'

This last report was soon followed by a competition to design the building, which was won by T. B. Silcox from Bath, though building work did not commence until 1899. And then, finally, on 28 October 1899, forty-six years after the first newspaper report:

> Llandudno New Town Hall: the ceremony of placing the memorial stone of the New Municipal Buildings by the Right Hon. Lord Mostyn, who generously gave the site on which the new municipal home is being erected in Lloyd Street. The old Board of Improvement Commissioners frequently complained strongly, of the highly unsatisfactory premises in which the town's affairs are at present conducted. These grumblings of the 'City Fathers' have not decreased since the local authority acquired the dignity of an Urban District Council.

Llandudno town hall represents an example of neo-baroque architecture, reviving the designs of Christopher Wren in the late seventeenth and early eighteenth centuries, his most famous being St Paul's Cathedral in London. The design of contrasting white stone and red brick mirrors that of Chelsea town hall, built in 1885–87. Internally there is a large public hall with seating for 250; the council chambers are now home to Llandudno Town Council. It also houses the local Registry Office.

40. Emmanuel Christian Centre, Lloyd Street, Llandudno

The Emmanuel Christian Centre was built in 1908–09 as the Ebenezer Wesleyan Methodist Chapel, replacing two earlier – and smaller - chapels. Designed by William Beddoe Rees of Cardiff, Pevsner's *Architectural Guide* calls it 'one of the most notable chapel designs in Wales', and it has been described elsewhere as Rees' 'masterpiece'. It is square outside but has a round interior, an unusual feature: it is one of only two surviving 'round' chapels in Wales. Its red-brick exterior with sandstone embellishments and its lead dome and cupola are classical in style and it was planned to complement the adjacent town hall (built in 1901).

Wesleyan Methodists sometimes call the period from 1850 to the early 1900s the 'Age of Mahogany' – in fact, little actual mahogany was used, but the chapel interiors were becoming increasingly lavish to correspond with the dramatic and attention-grabbing

Emmanuel Christian Centre.

façades fashionable in this period. These opulent Nonconformist chapels were sometimes called 'Palaces of the Oral Arts', to reflect the importance and loquacity of the preaching held within: an anonymous actor visiting Wales in the early twentieth century commented, 'inside one is aware of the truly dramatic atmosphere of so many of the Welsh chapels which have an intimacy which brings together actor and audience or pastor and flock, closely locked together in the business of drama or worship – or both.'

When the lease from Mostyn Estates on the chapel expired in 1972, the Methodists moved to a smaller building. Ebenezer Chapel became vandalised, but it was refurbished and leased to the Emmanuel Pentecostal Church, and has been running as the Emmanuel Christian Centre since 1988.

41. The Close, Llanfairfechan

The Arts and Crafts Movement began in Britain around 1880 and quickly spread across Europe and America. Born of ideals, it grew out of a concern for the effects of industrialisation on traditional skills and design, as well as the lives of ordinary people. It pioneered new approaches to design and the decorative arts, on all levels and across a broad demographic; one of its philosophies was to turn the home into a work of art in its own right. Its two most influential figures in Britain were the designer and writer William Morris and the theorist and critic John Ruskin. Morris put Ruskin's philosophies on the relationship between art, society and labour into practice through his emphasis on the value of craftsmanship and the beauty of natural materials.

Herbert Luck North (1871–1941) was an acclaimed Arts and Crafts architect who lived and worked in Llanfairfechan from around 1901. The village contains the biggest concentration of his buildings, most notably The Close: a collection of twenty-five houses

Above: The Close.

Below: From a sales brochure of 1926, a house on The Close.

A COTTAGE AT LLANFAIRFECHAN, NORTH WALES.   HERBERT L. NORTH, F.R.I.B.A.,
Plans and Entrance Front.   *Architect.*

Clare's Department Store.

built on family land, all but one of which were designed by North. The earliest houses were built before the First World War; three small double-gabled houses were built in 1922 and seven larger houses with verandas followed in 1925. The rest of the site was developed between 1926 and 1940, with the final house designed after North's death by his partner and son-in-law P. M. Padmore. Most of the houses were built for specific clients, and although there are discernible changes in design as the build dates progress, all display distinctive Arts and Crafts characteristics such as white roughcast walls, Welsh slate roofs, cottage-style casement windows and steep gables. Traditional features such as exposed ceiling beams and inglenook fireplaces are also inside the houses. Each house in The Close is listed, and in 1989 the entire estate was designated a Conservation Area.

42. Clare's Department Store, Mostyn Street, Llandudno

Mostyn Street is Llandudno's most important commercial street; it was this area of the town that was the first to be developed in its reincarnation as a seaside holiday resort.

The original building, where Clare's now stands, was probably built in the late nineteenth century. At the turn of the century it was occupied by Arthurs Pioneer Stores and was taken over in the early part of the twentieth century by W. S. Williams, a local businessman who owned a variety of commercial concerns including a mill in Dolgellau. Williams ran his Llandudno shop as a drapery, selling a variety of goods including fabrics spun at his Dolgellau factory. In 1926 the premises were taken over by Robert Clare Baxter, a draper originally from Runcorn, Cheshire. Robert rebuilt the shop with an art deco classical façade and renamed it Clare's Modern Store, a high-class ladies' dressmakers and milliners; over time, other departments such as china, cutlery and glass, kitchenware, electrical goods, furniture and carpets were added.

After Robert's death in 1950 the shop continued to be run by his son, and later by his two grandchildren. Clare's is unusual in Llandudno because it has kept its traditional curved glass display windows rather than replacing them with the ubiquitous featureless plate glass so beloved of the 1960s and beyond. The shop also retains its ornate iron cage lift. The pneumatic tube money transfer system was only removed in 2002 when the shop was taken over by Ulster Stores.

43. Palace Cinema, High Street, Conwy

A map of Conwy, dated 1936, shows the Metropolitan Bank directly opposite the Castle Hotel on the High Street. This was inaccurate, for on 6 January that year the Palace Cinema had opened, built on the site of the bank. On offer that opening night was a showing of the newly released film *Lieutenant Daring RN* starring Hugh Williams: a tale of tense drama on the high seas, complete with Chinese pirates capturing the heroine, Geraldine Fitzgerald, and her brave rescue by our hero.

At the beginning of the nineteenth century a number of private banks were set up across Britain, especially in newly industrialised towns. They were founded to serve the needs of industry and invested money in projects such as transport systems, canals and turnpike roads. Unfortunately, these banks could make bad investments and change hands several

Former Palace Cinema, designed to be in keeping with its surroundings, end gables paying homage to close neighbour Plas Mawr. *Inset*: Wall plaque, former Palace cinema.

times. The North and south Wales Bank, for example, was taken over by Midland Bank in 1908. It had been in trouble in 1847 and employee Hugh Pugh set up the Pwllheli District Bank. It eventually became Pugh Jones and Company of Pwllheli, also known as Caernarvonshire and District Bank, with a branch on the High Street in Conwy. Another bank, the grandly named National Bank of Wales Ltd, had been set up in 1879; by 1891 it had taken over the bank of Hugh Pugh and Company. But all was not going well, and two years later they were taken over by the Metropolitan Bank.

The cinema was built on the bank's site in 1935, to a design by architect Sydney Colwyn Foulkes, for independent operator H. Christmas Jones. Later that year, the cinema gained the 'Cinema of the Year Award'; Mr Foulkes was granted the 'Special Design Award'. The auditorium block was large and rather plain but the lighting was spectacular, and could bathe the auditorium with over 400 tints and colours. It was given an apt 1930s name, 'Holophane'. The ceiling dome onto which the Holophane played was unadorned; on either side of the proscenium stood six silvered columns which acted as reflectors, as did the silvered panels showing the faces of leading film stars of the time. All of which must have given a stunning light-show – one that predated those found in 1970s discos by forty years.

By the 1970s the owners were diversifying the attractions on offer and stage shows were occasionally presented. The cinema closed in the early 1980s and was replaced by a bingo hall, which in turn closed in early 2013.

44. The Round House, Glan-y-Mor Road, Llandudno Junction

The Round House, one of the few remaining non-residential art deco buildings in the area, is a fine example of the later period of the style, 'streamline moderne'. Very popular in the 1920s and '30s, it is characterised by curving forms and long horizontal lines.

Designed by renowned and prolific local architect Sidney Colwyn Foulkes, the building was constructed at an estimated cost of £4,500 for use as Conwy Borough Council's new electricity centre. It was reported in the local press as resembling the façade of a modern

The Round House.

cinema, and was the 'largest and most up to date municipally-owned electricity showrooms and offices in north Wales'. It was officially opened on 30 June 1938 by the Mayor of Llandudno, Joseph T. Jones, to meet the demands of an increasing number of consumers in the area – when electricity was first distributed by the borough in 1924 there were 324 consumers who used 95,849 units of power. By the end of the financial year in 1938, this had risen to 2,709 consumers and 1,501,920 units

A report in the *North Wales Weekly News*, published on the day the new centre opened, states:

> That electricity is a boon everyone will agree. Among other things it gives you light, warms your rooms, supplies hot water, cooks your food, washes your clothing, cleans your carpets, gives you entertainment and drives your sewing machine. One only has to go back twenty years to realise the enormous stride that has been made in harnessing this wonderful force.

That electricity was still considered a rather new-fangled and exotic notion is evident in the sentence 'the public are especially invited to visit the meter room at the new showrooms, where meters are carefully tested before being put in use'. An elaborate opening ceremony involved the mayor, mayoress and deputy mayor, the chairman of the Electricity Committee, the official handing over of keys, an inscribed commemorative tablet and various speeches.

The property transferred to Manweb on the nationalisation of the electricity industry in 1948, becoming the headquarters and depot of Manweb's Conwy Valley district. It was disposed of in the 1970s and was used by a boat builders, as well as a temporary Justice Clerk's office while the new court house in Llandudno was being built. Since 2007 it has been owned by a local firm of chartered accountants.

45. Marl Cold Store, Llandudno Junction Industrial Estate

At the outbreak of the Second World War military concerns were not the only priority: provision also had to be made for the needs of the civilian population, including control of

Cubist-influenced Marl Cold Store.

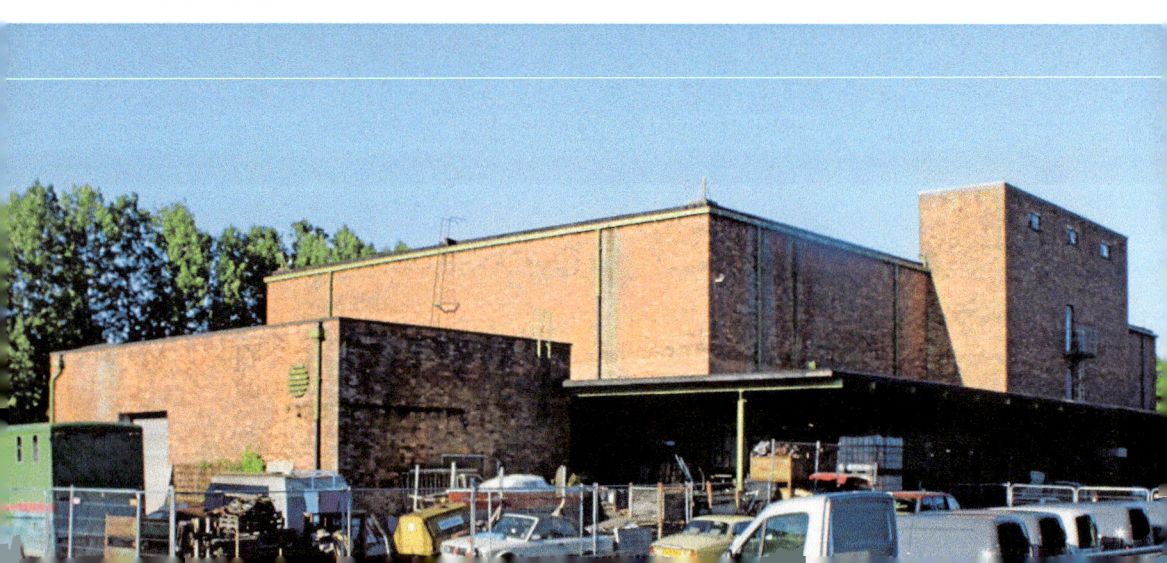

the economy and ensuring that the food supply was maintained and regulated. Before the war Britain had imported 55 million tons of food per month; after 1939 this dropped to 12 million tons. Petrol was soon rationed and by January 1940 so was bacon, sugar and butter, with other foodstuffs following as the costs of war became increasingly apparent. By June 1941 clothing was being rationed and 'hand-me-downs' came into their own.

As well as ensuring that food was available the government had to plan for its distribution, and the Ministry of Food set up nearly fifty refrigerated storage depots around the country. Marl Cold Store was one of these, built in 1939. These buildings were often connected to the rail network, ensuring that food could be transported in bulk and distribution could be more easily managed. Marl Cold Store was linked to the Chester and Holyhead main line by the 'Marl Siding'. The building is decidedly functional, almost Cubist in its design. It measures 63.7 by 43.1 metres, a vast structure constructed of brick around a framework of insulated steel.

At the end of the Second World War another war broke out, though one of a very different nature: the Cold War. During the previous hostilities the USA and the Soviet Union had been allies, fighting against a common enemy. However, longstanding tensions and grievances surfaced between the two powers and these quickly turned into overwhelming distrust and animosity, including the threat of nuclear war. Into this Cold War were thrust allies of the two powers, including Britain. To counter this threat, regional centres were designated, which could serve as headquarters for local government. It was proposed that Marl Cold Store should be adapted for this purpose, to be the Home Office's Regional Government Headquarters (RGHQ) for north Wales, though the building was never converted for this purpose.

46. Royal Artillery School, Great Orme, Llandudno

Despite the successful exploits of the RAF and their allies during the Battle of Britain in July to October 1940, the south-east of Britain remained vulnerable to bombing and further threats of attack and invasion by Hitler's forces. As a consequence, much of the infrastructure of war transferred to less assailable locations: the Royal Artillery School relocated from Shoeburyness in Essex in September 1940. Many sites on the west coast of Britain were considered before opting for an area on the west shore of the Great Orme, chosen because target vessels could be anchored offshore in the Menai Straits, and conditions were good for directing ships by radio. Designed by the Royal Engineers, the layout of the site was planned in just one day, using toy balloons bought locally as site markers.

As well as a gunnery wing, wireless and searchlight wings were set up in 1940; the school trained officers and other ranks in the art of coast artillery and radar technology, and assisted in the development of new weaponry, instrumentation and tactics. Officer cadet courses began in 1941 and reached a peak in 1942, when 150 officers, 115 cadets and 445 other ranks could be taken in, and as many as fourteen courses could be run simultaneously. Many other local buildings were also used by the Coast Artillery School, including nearby hotels. The school's staff also participated in joint exercises with the Llandudno Home Guard and the RAF, who had a radar installation at the Great Orme Summit Hotel. Red flags were hoisted around the area, including at Llandudno lighthouse

Above: Royal Artillery School, Great Orme. The electricity generating station: this contained three generators powered by Lister engines. Because the searchlights used a large amount of electric power, connection direct to the Llandudno UDC mains was not appropriate as the surge would have had adverse effects on the town's supply.

Below: Set in a dramatic location, three traversable searchlight positions. The searchlights could be adjusted so the beams could follow targets.

and West Shore bathing pool, to indicate when firing was taking place. Bye-laws introduced in 1942 prohibited the public from entering the foreshore of the firing range or taking vessels into the sea.

The gunneries stretch for a kilometre along the coast and were in full use until the end of the war, when the arms and equipment were removed and the land returned to Mostyn Estates. The buildings became derelict and most were demolished in the mid-1950s and 1960s under an official clearance scheme. However, the foundations of some of the buildings and installations have survived, and in 2011 the site was scheduled by Cadw as an ancient monument in recognition of its historical significance.

47. Parisella's Ice-Cream Kiosk, The Quay, Conwy

In a book focussed on the history of majestic or significant buildings, it is perhaps easy to forget that visitors to Conwy often enjoy other highlights traditionally associated with seaside resorts. One such highlight is tucking into an ice cream on a hot summer's day. Parisella's ice-cream kiosk has been a popular feature of Conwy's quay since the early 1970s.

With the massive rise in European population following the Industrial Revolution, migration accelerated – millions, for example, left Europe to start a new life in North America. Closer to home, movement within Europe became more commonplace as people sought a better life and new opportunities. Italian migration to Britain began in the eighteenth century. As with most migrants, they turned their hand to whatever work was

Parisella's ice-cream kiosk on a sunny summer's day.

Service with a smile in the Continental Ice Cream Parlour, No. 6 Lancaster Square, c. 1955. Irena (Aunty Irene) in the centre; to the left, Mrs Lavelle, from Berwick upon Tweed; to the right, Nancy Hughes. (Courtesy of Tony Parisella)

available: many worked in ports, but by the close of the nineteenth century the British were being introduced to traditional Italian cooking – and Italian-made ice cream.

Domenico Parisella was one who sought to better his prospects in a new land. In 1912, aged just sixteen, he left the village of Colle San Magno in Lazio, and emigrated to Britain. Initially he settled in the Scottish town of Greenock, learning ice cream making with the Di Murro family's catering firm. By 1936 he had moved across the border with his wife Carolina Forte and their three children, Leo, Irena and Joseph, to Berwick-on-Tweed, where he set up a shop selling fish and chips in the winter months and home-made ice cream in the summer. Seven years later they moved to north Wales where Domenico continued making ice cream, this time for Forte's of Llandudno.

In 1949, he set up his own business in Conwy: the Continental Ice Cream Parlour in Lancaster Square. Although by 1953 ice cream was still being sold in Wales from horse-drawn carts, Domenico had purchased a motorised tricycle for his deliveries. Throughout the 1950s and '60s the business went from strength to strength: Domenico making the ice cream in a vertical freezer at the rear of the shop, Leo, Joe and Irena's husband Arthur driving the vans across north Wales, and Irena – under the watchful eye of Carolina – running the parlour. A true family-run business, from manufacture through distribution, to direct retail.

In the early 1970s, a new plant that could produce 130 gallons of ice cream every hour was installed to cope with increased orders – the wholesale business had by now expanded to include the West Midlands and Kent. The early 1970s saw Parisella's take over the kiosk on the quay from Hi Hat Ices of Llandudno, who took it over from the council in the 1960s. Domenico died in May 1976, leaving a legacy of ice cream making which his family continue to this day.

In 2006, under the direction of Joe, with son Tony and his daughter Emma, a new factory producing artisan ice cream and sorbet was commissioned, serving not just the family's parlour on the High Street and the kiosk on the quay, but over ninety other outlets across north Wales and England.

48. Royal Cambrian Academy, Crown Lane, Conwy

Ever since the late eighteenth century, British artists of international fame had been drawn by the wild beauty of north Wales. By the latter half of the nineteenth century, political unrest in Europe had made the traditional European Grand Tour unwise, and a group of English artists had settled in the Conwy Valley, enabled by the spread of the railways to travel there with greater ease. By the 1880s the area was at the peak of its fame as a home for large numbers of professional and amateur artists. Membership of the group grew to around forty; it was instrumental in founding the Cambrian Academy with like-minded Welsh artists.

Originally based in Llandudno Junction, official recognition came quickly when Queen Victoria commanded that the Academy be styled as 'Royal' in 1882. Four years later, local landowner Lord Mostyn offered them the lease of his neglected Elizabethan mansion, Plas Mawr, in Conwy, which the Academicians restored, making it one of the outstanding examples of Elizabethan architecture in Britain. However, although it was an elegant home for the Academy it did not make a good gallery, and in 1896 the Victoria Gallery annexe

Left: Royal Cambrian Academy of Art.

Right: Plas Mawr – looking like some TLC wouldn't go amiss – advertising the Royal Cambrian Academy of Art's Summer Exhibition.

was constructed to extend the hanging space. Work from non-members was now included in the exhibitions and the Annual Summer Exhibition began.

In 1994, the Academy broke its connection with Plas Mawr and moved to its current home, a purpose-built gallery adjacent to the mansion. The Academy holds nine exhibitions per year and has a significant and extensive education programme; former presidents include eminent Welsh artists Augustus John and Kyffin Williams, and its patron is HRH the Prince of Wales.

49. Venue Cymru, The Promenade, Llandudno

Although Venue Cymru is one of the few obviously modern buildings along Llandudno's promenade, there has been a theatre on the site since 1894. Originally named the Victoria Palace, it was intended as a temporary structure as part of a project that was to have included a second pier to serve Craig-y-Don, at the eastern end of Llandudno Bay. However, this project never materialised, and the theatre became a permanent landmark for over 100 years.

By 1895 it had been renamed Rivière's Concert Hall, when French musician Jules Rivière based himself there after falling out with the management of the Pier Pavilion; under Riviere's baton the name changed briefly to the Llandudno Opera House. In 1900, Jules Rivière was enticed away to Colwyn Bay's newly opened Victoria Pier, and the theatre was renamed the Hippodrome; it continued to be used as a concert venue during the summer season, and as a roller-skating rink and ballroom (presumably not simultaneously) during the winter months. In 1915, it was bought by theatre impresario Will Catlin. It opened in June 1916 as the Arcadia and was the home of Catlin's Pierrots, which later became Catlin's Follies. This traditional seaside entertainment was extremely popular with holidaymakers, and the theatre continued to flourish, even surviving Will Catlin's death in 1953. It continued to be run by Catlin's family until it was bought by Llandudno Urban Council in 1968.

In 1982, the Aberconwy Centre – a conference centre with space for 1,000 delegates – opened next door to the Arcadia. Meanwhile, the theatre's fortunes were steadily declining, and on 22 June 1994 its curtain fell for the last time. In the same year the Aberconwy Centre was extended and developed, and renamed the north Wales Theatre and Conference Centre. The new state-of-the-art theatre had a 1,500-seat auditorium and was able to stage the largest of West End touring productions. The Arcadia lay abandoned and derelict until July 2005, when a £10.7-million project began to enhance and redevelop the facilities next door. The Arcadia was demolished and a new conference atrium and suite of meeting and conference rooms were built where it had stood. This new development included a 1,550 square metre arena, dramatically raising the total capacity of the conference centre to over 5,000. The western extension added a café bar, restaurant, box office and office space. The new north Wales Theatre, Conference Centre and Arena proved something of a mouthful, so a competition was launched in 2005 in a local newspaper to rename the complex. The winning entry Venue Cymru was chosen a few months later; it was officially opened on 15 January 2007.

Venue Cymru. *Inset*: Wartime programme for 'Caitlin's Follies, Summer Show Supreme', presenting a wide range of variety acts including The Sherry Brothers 'in one of their Famous Cocktails'.

The exterior design of the building was controversial throughout all the planning stages from 1981 onwards, with some critics complaining that the design should have reflected the town's Victorian heritage (Pevsner's *Architectural Guide* describes it as 'emphatically horizontal'). However, whatever one's thoughts on the architecture, there is no doubt that Venue Cymru's facilities have proved a valuable addition not just to Llandudno, but to the whole of north Wales.

50. Porth Eirias, The Promenade, Colwyn Bay

Our final building brings together two themes that have permeated many previous entries: the area's relationship with the sea and its attraction for visitors (some, such as Edward I, were probably not made as welcome as most have been). The venture was predicated on improving the promenade's coastal defences together with continuing regeneration works to further the economic development of the town.

A design competition jointly supported by the Welsh Assembly and the European Regional Development Fund was held in 2011, and the winning design was proposed by Liverpool-based K2 Architects. Although this design was a finalist in the 2014 Wales Awards for Regeneration held by the Royal Institution of Chartered Surveyors, it did not find favour in all quarters, especially, perhaps, as the completed building departed in certain aspects from the original design entry.

The centre opened in May 2013 accompanied by a two-day music festival, with the official opening by the First Minister of Wales taking place that September. A restaurant/bistro opened in July 2015.

One of the main functions of the centre is to provide for those who enjoy the sea. Based at Porth Eirias, Colwyn Bay Watersports offer training and tailored courses for groups and individuals, both locals and visitors alike, including powerboating, windsurfing and sailing, as well as hiring out various small craft. Other amenities at the centre comprise changing facilities, a meeting and event space and an outdoor children's playground.

Thus, two themes which began in the earliest periods – strong links with the sea and embracing visitors – remain as important as ever in Conwy and around.

Porth Eirias.

Acknowledgements

For permission to use photographs and other illustrations, we thank: Dave and Karen Alexander; CADW / Welsh Government; Castle Hotel, Conwy; National Library of Wales; National Portrait Gallery, London; Tony Parisella; Dennis Roberts and Penmaenmawr Museum; St Paul's Church, Craig-y-Don. Copyrights as indicated in accompanying captions.

For permission to take other photographs and for offering invaluable information we thank:
Helen Barritt and Conwy Town Council
Bodysgallen Hall
Castle Hotel, Conwy
Bill Chapman (Conwy Town Council)
Huw Davies and Rachael Gill (Conwy County Borough Council)
Philip Evans
Dilys Glynn (St Benedict's Church, Gyffin)
Deborah Haigh-Roberts (St Paul's Church, Craig-y-Don)
Richard Cynan Jones (Oriel Mostyn Gallery)
Dave Manton
Tony Parisella
The staff of Plas Mawr, Conwy
Dennis Roberts
Tracey Roscoe (St David's College)
Carolyn Sherlock and St Mary's Church, Conwy
Syrinx Recorder Consort
Richard Thomas and Mostyn Estates Ltd

Also Available from Amberley Publishing

CONWY & DISTRICT PUBS
PETER JOHNSON & CATHERINE JEFFERIS

Raise a glass with Peter Johnson and Catherine Jefferis as they trace some of the many charming pubs in and around Conwy.

978 1 4456 5312 9

Available to order direct 01453 847 800

www.amberley-books.com